ALIVE
and
STILL
KICKING

ALIVE
and
STILL
KICKING

Terry Gordon

ALIVE AND STILL KICKING

iUniverse books may be ordered through booksellers or by contacting:

iUniverse
1663 Liberty Drive
Bloomington, IN 47403
www.iuniverse.com
844-349-9409

Because of the dynamic nature of the Internet, any web addresses or links contained in this book may have changed since publication and may no longer be valid. The views expressed in this work are solely those of the author and do not necessarily reflect the views of the publisher, and the publisher hereby disclaims any responsibility for them.

Any people depicted in stock imagery provided by Getty Images are models, and such images are being used for illustrative purposes only. Certain stock imagery © Getty Images.

ISBN: 978-1-6632-4012-5 (sc)
ISBN: 978-1-6632-4013-2 (e)

Library of Congress Control Number: 2022909556

Print information available on the last page.

iUniverse rev. date: 05/21/2022

Contents

Thoughts to Ponder

My mother was taken from me due to cancer in October 1964, which was less than two months after my twelfth birthday. During the time that my mother and I were together, she taught me so much about life simply by being a mother and leading by example. She always taught with love and compassion, both of which I miss from her still today.

She was always there when something happened, good or bad. Mom and I bowled together in mother and son tournaments, and we always came home with a trophy. Sunday dinners were a favourite time of the week because that was where we would sit down and talk about the week's happenings over my favourite dinner, which would be mashed potatoes with gravy alongside roast beef and dinner rolls. For dessert, it was vanilla ice cream. They're still my favourites today. Mom was also there at the hospital waiting for me to arrive by ambulance after I almost drowned from a school outing at a neighbouring outdoor pool. Honestly, she was my best friend back then. I still miss the loving and warm hugs that always meant so much.

I do have one regret that still haunts me to this day. One day, she sat me down and mentioned that her wish for me was to become a priest. I told her I would think about it and let her know one way or another. Unfortunately, I never had the opportunity to tell her before God took her from me. I did not want to disappoint or upset her by telling her that I would not follow that path, but I did want to tell her before she died. On top of that, my family thought it would be best to keep me away during her last hours, which was painfully upsetting to me. Not only did I not have the opportunity to say that I could not follow her wish, but also I did not have the opportunity of one last hug and one last "I love you." I still carry that pain with me today.

Throughout my life of good times, bad times, and challenging times, I have concluded that my mother is still present in my life. There have been times when I feel a gentle breeze touch my face or what feels like a gentle hand on my shoulder. It may sound strange, but I swear Mom is still looking out for me. Maybe that is the reason God took her from me. He had other plans for her. All I know is it is comforting to have her presence because it means it's only a matter of time until we are together again. Don't get me wrong; I am going to be kicking and scratching to stay here, but when the time comes to go, I know that once again my mother will be there, waiting for me with open arms, which is very comforting to know.

Until then, I will do my best to be a better person each and every day, as Mom would want me to be. And yes, Mom, I still have the Bible you gave me when you sent me off to Sunday school. It is on a shelf, and I see it every day, which reassures me that I am in a safe place with you near. I will bring it with me when we get together, and I know that you will not be upset when you see a few tattered pages.

Acknowledgements

Marybel Unabia

Marybel is a very outgoing and caring person with a very positive attitude towards others and life in general. She always looks for the positive and bright side of any day. Marybel has a way of making my day a better one, no matter the situation. She has inspired me to follow my dreams, which kick-started me to follow those dreams with my wildlife safaris.

She encourages me constantly to do things that make me happy. She is a hard-working person who does everything from her heart and not for recognition. If there is a way to help someone, Marybel will make it happen. We all should be so humble and giving. I am forever grateful.

Elena Buksha

I would like to thank Elena not only for her timely picture, which is proudly shown on the cover of my book, but also for making my life a lot easier with less stress at work. Along with her impeccable work ethics, organizational skills, and consideration for co-workers, she has a terrific sense of humour and a zest for life.

Antonietta

I honestly don't know what Antonietta cannot do once her mind is set. She can do three to four things at a time—and accurately, I might add.

Along with that, Antonietta and her mother have a home baking business that is second to none. They are the best baked goods I have ever tasted.

When Antonietta volunteered to do the task of typing my manuscript, I was overwhelmed with relief, to say the least. Not knowing the size of the project didn't faze or deter her. She wanted to help. But after all, this is Antonietta I am talking about, so I should not be surprised and will humbly say thank you.

The Reasons Why

As I look out at the freshly decorated and picturesque landscape, it has suddenly come to my attention that complaining about all the snow shovelling that was done earlier this morning reminds me of my age (I am not getting any younger, you know), and although the body parts feel the exertion of pushing and lifting show for an hour or so, it seems to be worth every ache and pain.

What I mean to say is just smelling the fresh air, tasting a few snowflakes that fall gently from above, and looking at the surreal setting with the beauty, innocence, and cleanliness of the day that only one could imagine made my reflection of the day seem more meaningful, which meant that I was able to put more into my thoughts.

For your information, I try to take a few minutes at the end of every day to reflect on the day's events to see what I did and did not accomplish, what I did and did not say, to make tomorrow a better day not just for myself but also for those close to me. That includes anyone that I have a chance to say hello to during my day.

To me, these reflections are a very simple yet necessary and positive way to make the next day a better one for all. Life is so short, so why not enjoy and share every single moment of every day with others who cross our path, giving them all love, laughter, humility, and respect? We all deserve it, and as the old adage goes, "Do unto others as you would have them do unto you," which is also known as the "golden rule—or as I put on the back cover of my first book, *Every Day's a Good Day*, "To receive love, respect, and understanding, you must first give the same." It's that simple. Life is not an automatic get-out-of-jail card for a pain-free, "do and get what you want" way of life. There are going to be obstacles, challenges, setbacks, and pain that we all will encounter during our lives.

To me, life is a privilege, and we are our own makers; one way or another, we make the journey a good one or not. How many times have you heard the line "He's his own worst enemy"? Please don't forget that life can be snatched away in a moment's notice. That is why I try to make sure I make a positive impact on those whom I had a chance to encounter. It could be as simple as a smile, handshake, hug, or friendly greeting. Never, and I mean never, go to bed with anger in your heart or on your mind about something that happened earlier during the day. You will regret it. I know that I have. Those feelings and words leave an impact on those of whom you directed them to, and as a reminder, words do hurt and cannot be taken back. If you can honestly answer the following statement with positivity, then it has been a good day: "At the end of my day, I reflect, and if I knowingly have not hurt anyone physically, emotionally, and financially, then that allows me to be at peace with myself."

Each and every one of us can improve, whether it's through kinder words, thoughtful actions to those around us, or ignoring and not getting involved with anger and resentment in reactions from others who are not having a good day or are plain ignorant. It is not worth the effort to get involved with negativity and add fuel to the fire. Rather, one should try to de-escalate the situation, if one is forced to be involved. I guess by now you have figured out that I watch far too many police shows, to use the word *de-escalate* so eagerly.

You would be surprised—no, emphatically amazed—by the reward of your giving and helping others. The simple gesture of holding a door open for someone or a friendly and sincere greeting to a total stranger can make the difference in whether it is a good day or a not-so-good day. That is rewarding not only for the stranger you came across but also for you. Don't forget that it adds to your few moments of reflection at day's end, and that has to make you smile and feel good about yourself and your day.

Learning is also key to enjoying a good day. If anyone tells you that they have all the knowledge they need or that they know it all, I will simply be right to the point and emphasize that they are full of shit. To me, that is a sign of ignorance and arrogance. Maybe they are insecure about themselves, or maybe they really don't have the intellect to learn. But of course, they will deny that, so once again, walk away or try to de-escalate—a word so nice, I have now said it twice.

There is a myth out there that humans only use 10 per cent of their brain, and I have a few names in mind that would back that up, but due to legalities, I will keep those names to myself. I know that it is just a myth and may not be accurate, but it does give you an idea of how much we can learn. Wouldn't it be nice to put that learning to good use?

My way to learn is through observation. You know—keep your mouth closed, and keep your eyes and ears open. Take off the blinders and observe what is all around you. As an example, instead of driving from point A to point B in a reckless manner, which includes speeding to get you there faster and often putting others in peril with your lack of consideration or skills as a driver, try on your route what I have learned on my drive from my home to my office. Yours would be different obviously, but nevertheless it can be achieved if you put your mind to it. For your information, driving from my home in Alliston to my office in Bolton takes approximately thirty-five minutes for a nearly forty-kilometre drive. I have discovered the following on more than one occasion.

1) Deer crossing (must be careful so as to not hit them)
2) Horses frolicking in the fields
3) Cows grazing
4) Hawks on hydro poles or flying over the fields, looking for prey
5) Birds flying alongside their hatchlings
6) Children with smiles getting off the school bus
7) Slithering snakes on the shoulder of the road
8) Precision work of snowplough operators making our roads safe
9) Recycling bins (my way of observing who is trying to help the environment)

10) Anxious parents waiting for their children to arrive home safely from school
11) Frozen ponds in winter, with the young and the old skating on them
12) Large farm machines doing their daily chores
13) Unique businesses that advertise their specialty from their home
14) Entrance to small parks and trails (I should stop one time and investigate)
15) Tall, thin, mature trees that withstand all that Mother Nature throws at them
16) Small town with main street stores
17) Colours of trees (especially in the fall)
18) Discovery of a crop in a farmer's field (maybe on my plate in a few days)
19) Watching children play in the park near my home
20) Watching the colours of a sunrise going to work or a sunset coming home (everyone is different from the next)
21) Cleanliness and serenity of a snowfall glistening under the sun's rays

I truly enjoy watching the above mentioned repeatedly. All of those scenarios are just in my commute to and from the office every day. I am sure everyone has similar settings, and if they would just stop and smell the roses, wouldn't that make their day better, not to mention make life more rewarding?

So you see, maybe if we took time to look at the little things of beauty in life, we would not worry as much about the larger things in life, or maybe we would be able to cope better. Either way, I know that I am trying to make my days better, which leads me to the reason why my days are getting better one day at a time. I look at the little things, and how can I forget to mention the biggest challenge that we all face today, the COVID-19 pandemic? That has truly put life in perspective and shown all of us just how frail life can be. I mean, just look at the people worldwide, young and old, who have not only lost their lives to COVID but also have died while being alone. No one is immune to this horrific disease, and the sooner it's under control, the better.

I hope that people learn how fragile life can be and to appreciate not only what we have but also the freedom we have to enjoy our blessed lives. But I have my doubts. I pray that those with mental issues and depression can get through this ordeal. Also, while on the same topic, my heart goes out to each and every healthcare worker during this difficult and challenging time. To the doctors, nurses, paramedics, registration clerks, housekeeping, security, and more, a heartfelt and sincere thank-you, and wish I could give a hug to each and every person involved. You truly have my respect and appreciation for your professionalism and hard work. I can only imagine what your days are like physically and emotionally.

I mentioned in my first book how much I love, support, and respect nurses. That was back in 2016, which was long before the pandemic, under the title *Nurses Are the Best*. The following bathroom reader–style stories were accumulated over the past year or so out of curiosity, observation, or because of my response to the stupidity or ignorance of others. So as not to break tradition from my previous writings, they are in alphabetical order again, with the only difference being that this time around, I have not separated the titles in "Thoughts to Ponder" and "Thoughts to Ponder (on the Lighter Side)". That will be left to your imagination, because your interpretation may be different from another person's. Plus, I may be getting lazy.

My family, friends, and co-workers can attest to these stories, of which I include myself more than enough times on my own personal mix-ups, miscues, or screw-ups. If you can't laugh at yourself, whom can you laugh at? There are probably a handful of people close to me who will probably tell you that I should be wearing a white jacket with the arms tied at the back, but that's another story for a later time. These short stories are here because they helped me get through the dark times, and to be quite honest, they still exist, although they are getting less frequent as time goes on.

I promised myself to not bring up the past because that was done previously, so I will leave that be. These writings are done to hopefully put a smile on your face and to embrace life through human feelings or human traits as itemized below. We all have them so let's put them to good use.

1) Warmth
2) Loving
3) Caring
4) Respect
5) Humility
6) Giving
7) Compassion
8) Honesty
9) Non-judgemental
10) Humour

If we all did a little to help others by listening, giving, and being respectful, can you imagine how happy we can make this world? Along with a little laughter, the rewards would be priceless.

I hope that this has come across to everyone as I meant it to, especially to my children, Jason, Nicholas, Andrew, and Jennifer.

THOUGHTS
TO PONDER

Annoying Bumper Stickers

Please tell me that I am not alone when I mention that most bumper stickers on vehicles are not only extremely annoying but also very much an eyesore. They tell me that the insecure person looking for attention has no taste for class or any respect for the looks of the vehicle. They are tacky, to say the least, but are also close to criminal, with a few of them close to crossing the line of sanity. The ones I have witnessed and noted below in my summary of the most obnoxious and annoying bumper stickers will back up my conclusion that in general, I think you should simply stay clear of these drivers because I honestly feel they need help and should seek out some sort of therapy.

It should also be noted that the same could be said for people posting services on paper and then sticking them to a community mailbox, or cardboard signs stapled to anything wood advertising garage sales. For those who do it, let it be known that I don't tolerate that crap and do not hesitate to take the posting down if I happen to pass by. I wish the idiots would do the same and take down all the postings of the garage sale after it's over.

The following bumper stickers and postings are ones that I see from time to time, as well as a few that were mentioned to me by friends. They are annoying, to say the least.

	COMMENT
I Don't Run	Tells the world you don't exercise, mocking those who do.
Please be patient, student driver	Might make you cautious and courteous if it was a real student, but on your own car? Not funny.
Certified Wacko	Only two words, but it says a lot about the person behind the wheel. Would not want to be in front or behind this vehicle in traffic.
I hate people	I get it; we all have those days. But chances are this driver will cut you off in traffic, give you the finger, or both.
My kid can beat up your honour student	Violence is not funny, so why advertise it on your vehicle? It looks like you're trying to pick a fight.
This vehicle stops at all garage sales	A lot of starts and stops, so stay clear. FYI, I don't like garage sales.
Nobody cares about your stick figure family [shows a car hitting a stick figure]	Although stick-figure family bumper stickers are so yesterday, this is a bit much because accidents are not funny.
I pooped today	Not much to say about this sticker. Why?

Other Ones Worth Noting as Annoying

Back off, please! You're annoying my car.
Silly boys, trucks are for girls.
Powered by Jesus.
If you can read this, you're too close.
Horn broke—watch for finger.
The closer you get, the slower I go.
I bet Jesus would have used his turn signals.
I have Jesus. He's in the trunk.
Stick family diagrams.
Are we there yet? Are we there yet?
Baby on board.
No baby on board.

Former baby on board.

Garage sale with date and address (on poles and fences).

Cleaning services (on mailboxes).

Roof repair (on mailboxes).

Lawn cutting (on mailboxes and signs on the boulevards).

Babysitting (on mailboxes).

Landscaping services (on mailboxes and signs on boulevards).

Anxiety, Anger, Depression, and Mental Health

Individually, these words are scary enough if someone is going through some issues, but if put together, they can be downright troublesome, devastating, and deadly if not handled with the utmost compassion, understanding, and de-escalating tactics. That has become more evident with what is going on today in the streets. The police are not always to blame, as their training does not give them the tools to resolve psychological issues, so I will not go there. I have too much respect for the men and women in blue, although here are a few bad apples that unfortunately give everyone on the force a bad name. That does not seem fair considering every work environment has a few bad apples, but they are not in the public eye.

Everyone has issues once in a while, and I am no exception. For years, I used to carry my anger with me, which also let anxiety and depression join the club. As I mentioned in my first book, I thought of and attempted suicide three times between the ages of thirteen and seventeen. That's a thing of the past, and I will not mention those times again.

I would like to say that there should be more people trained to handle situations where anxiety, anger, and depression start to take over. I don't mean visiting a shrink (that covers a lot of people in that field) with a scheduled visit a few days after the fact. By that, it's like nothing happened and everyone is calm. I mean having someone who could be escorted to the scene alongside an officer for everyone's protection to try to de-escalate the situation. They should not add fuel to the fire by provocation but should add words of compassion and understanding.

This world needs more love and a lot less hate. Oh, by the way, no disrespect to the professionals who talk to you while you are in their cosy little therapy room at a rate of one hundred dollars per hour, but I don't trust them. Sometimes I think they have more issues than I do. In fact, I had one therapist who tried to tell my wife and me how to raise our children, and she did not have any kids of her own. How is that going to help? Every child is different, so the so-called books of raising children can all go out the window.

I have something better than books and therapists, and that's people who are great friends. If I need to talk about anything, I know they are there to listen twenty-four seven.

Bikes, Joggers, and Gyms

To be quite honest, exercising in an orderly fashion with respect to cycling, jogging, or weight lifting has never been in my repertoire, but then again, why should it be a necessity to have a happy, healthy, energetic, and meaningful life?

I have to admit that having a routine, no matter what you do, helps achieve what you set out to accomplish in the field of athleticism. It is also a good idea for life in general. But some people take it to extremes. Let me explain. If I wake up at 4:00 a.m., which seems to be a norm for me lately, and the weather permits, I may go for a leisurely walk for about an hour or so. But doing this on a regular basis rain or shine is not going to happen.

For some reason, joggers go at roughly the same time every day. And if jogging in a residential area, why must they go on the road where motorized vehicles travel? I asked a jogger about that one time, and he told me that the sidewalk is a challenge due to stepping on and off curbs, which is dangerous. My reply was being hit by a car is a little more dangerous. And what's with the funny headbands?

The same could be said of cyclists. They go in groups of as little as two and as many as twenty. Are they afraid of going at it alone, or is it an excuse to get out and pretend they are in a biker gang? Except instead of leather, they are wearing spandex with advertising, as if they have been sponsored by firms while they cycle around. In their minds, they seem to be in the Tour de France.

Added to that mix are the gymnasts, who are a breed on their own. I mean, why do you have to get up, get washed, get dressed, drive to the gym, get changed into your workout outfit, do your thing on the treadmill, do your thing with the weights, get showered, get changed again, and go home? I mean, hello? Just put on a pair of jogging pants, open your front door, and go for a walk or a jog. It is convenient and just as effective as going to the gym. Or if you want to get a little creative, put something together and carry it with you as a little workout with weights.

I have seen and heard people on TV complaining about the gyms being closed during the COVID-19 crisis. It sounds like an addiction that you have to go to the gym and that missing some time at the gym is like a drug addict not getting a fix. I have news for you, and that is I would rather stay safe from COVID than be exposed and have a chance of getting COVID. Just stop thinking of yourself and get creative in the meantime. It is only a (hopefully) temporary setback that we will go through. In short, just grow up.

Bleeding Hearts

There will probably be a lot of backlash with this, but for me, enough is enough. Every time you turn around, there seems to be another individual (or another group of people, or another generation of people) looking for sympathy for whatever happened, whether a long time ago or just recently. They are not just looking for an apology, recognition, or sympathy. One way or another, it ultimately boils down to money.

No matter how you cut it, the bottom line involves money and how much one can get. The media has just the platform to show it. I know there are things that happened years, decades, and centuries ago that bother me, but how is giving money to the cause going to fix the issue? It's not going to bring back the dead, and surely it will not erase what happened. What has happened cannot be undone, especially with money. To me, money is the root of all evil.

Why do people have to go this route just to make some money for nothing? But then again, money plays a part in almost everything we do. That's why I have no interest in giving money to any cause advertised over the media. If they can afford to pay exuberant prices for commercials, they can afford to help their own cause. I heard and read somewhere that some of these fundraisers—not all, but some—use up to ninety cents out of every dollar for their own costs like radio and TV time, wages, and rent. Hence, I do not give.

Then there are the GoFundMe sites on the internet. I saw one or two individuals trying to raise money for their own cause by pretending to have cancer and needing money for their bills and medicine, only to find out it was a scam. Hence, I do not give.

On top of that, ever since I saw on the news a few years back that a lady who was panhandling (begging for money) on Yonge Street finished for the day only to get up, walk to her car, and drive home. She did not walk to a shelter but drove home to a pretty good part of town. Another fraud. Hence, I do not give.

Recently, again on the idiot box, I witnessed a network asking for money because that's the only money they get (they claim) to promote their program. Have you seen some of the outfits they wear, the cars they drive, and the studios in which they work? To me, it looks like they should be the ones to give, not receive. Hence, I do not give.

There are even children among the adults going door to door and selling anything from chocolates to magazines to meat. They are not just trying to sell the product; a few almost beg with tears and say that this is the only money they receive for their starving families. Sorry, but I just do not buy it. Hence, I do not give.

It doesn't matter how much money you give or they get—it's never enough.

Before I forget, this one is just plain unacceptable but also funny at the same time. While in a shopping plaza parking lot one day, I was approached by a middle-aged woman with a sign that read, "I cannot speak English, but I need money for food for my children." After two or three feeble attempts to get in my face with the sign, I told her I do not give money to this sort of activity or something like that, and I continued to walk to my car. A few moments later, I heard her yell, "You prick. Go fuck yourself."

I then turned around and uttered, "I thought you couldn't speak English?" Her mouth dropped, and she mumbled something, turned around, and walked away with her tail between her legs. Hence, I do not give.

The last item in this story boggles my mind. There is a Black history month (which I find very interesting and love to learn about the history and culture) that happens in the month of February. There is an Asian Pacific American heritage month and older Americans month, which is in May; a gay and lesbian pride month in June; National Hispanic heritage month from mid-September to mid-October, National American Indian heritage month in November; and national women's history month and Irish American heritage month in April. These are just a few of the times set aside to celebrate and recognize cultures. I don't have a problem with any of these, but there is there not a month put out there for Canadian-born Canadians? I think that we could share some interesting stories related to history, religion, prominent Canadians, food, sports, dance, and more. Like I said in the beginning, there will probably be a few who will criticize what I have said, and that's OK. Everyone has a right to their opinion, and I respect their opinion. However, I do not think that I should apologize to anyone, and I am not even going to think about that at all. I give with my heart. If someone is in dire need of money for food, I will buy them food. If someone is in need of shelter, I will help bring them to a shelter. I have listened to their stories and shown them respect. If someone is cold and needs clothing for the outdoor extreme weather, I will provide them with gloves, toques, and sweaters. You see, I believe in helping the most vulnerable ones whom I can personally help, and I have done that by volunteering in one way or another over the past thirty years. At least I know where my money goes, and I personally get the satisfaction of helping someone in need. How many hypocrites who will criticize me have done volunteer work to help others like I and others have done? Not as many as I would like to see, I suspect. Let's help the ones near to us. We cannot control what others around the world go through due to the corruption of people, especially governments. The money rarely gets to those who need it, so give at home.

Brain Farts

With this title, I could go on for days on just my own personal scenarios. I mean, maybe it's because of my age that I notice more of what I did before, but more than likely it could be because of the increase in not-so-smart moves on my behalf, and maybe—no, probably—they are getting worse in complexity as well.

To give you an idea of what I am talking about, I have compiled a list of the most memorable brain farts that I can remember. They are not in any specific order, which means there is no scale of one to ten as to which ones are worse. I hope that I am not alone with some of these. If so, maybe I should consider seeking help, or maybe I should try to be a little more careful before committing a lot more than I do. Again, I emphasize that, thank goodness, I was gifted with a sense of humour.

1. Trying to find my cell phone in my office while putting drawings together and paperwork to take home to work (I love my job) at home. In my haste, when I could not find my phone, I managed to get my right hand free to dial my cell on the office phone, and when it rang, I discovered it in my left hand.
2. A handful of occasions taking out two clubs from my bag, one for the chip to the green and one for putting. I do that because my partner (also my best friend of over fifty years), Yasu, has a tendency to take off with the cart and look for his ball. Both Kiran and Nam (the other two gentlemen in our group) will vouch for me on that. A few holes later, I look once again for the wedge only

to discover that I left it a few holes back. Sometimes I get it back, and sometimes I don't.

3. Undoing the strap on the golf cart to get something out of the pocket of the bag and forgetting to put it back when getting in the cart to carry on. Guess what? Now I have to reverse my travels to pick up my bag and the clubs and balls that fall out.

I could be here all day with golf, but let's move on to other incidents.

4. Looking for my reading glasses and more often than not finding them on my head.
5. Wearing different socks. One time I wore two different shoes.
6. Leaving my cup of takeout coffee on top of the car while unlocking the door and then driving away and forgetting the coffee I had left on the car.
7. Somehow clicking the wrong key or keys on my keyboard while working on my drawings, only to have my computer screen reading everything not only upside down but also reversed. Thank goodness for the smarter people in my office to help me get out of the predicament.
8. Going to the office on the weekend to get work done for an upcoming deadline requirement only to forget the drawings or the USB stick with all my work on it. Once, I even forgot my key to get in.
9. Going to pay for an item in a store and then, at the cashier, realizing that my wallet or credit card was at home or in the car.
10. Walking up or down the stairs, and for some reason I seem to forget the number of steps, which means I trip over the top step or stomp on the floor thinking there is another step. Oftentimes, I have a coffee in my hand, which ultimately means I have a spill to clean up.
11. Going to the store on my way home to pick up two or three items and almost every time coming home forgetting one item that was to be bought.
12. After shopping, whether it be five minutes or five hours, forgetting where I parked the car. Sometimes I am so way off looking for it

that the alarm does not even help me. I don't ever want to mention the time I lost my car (or so I thought) at the airport. I found the spot where the car should have been, but one floor lower. It took me over an hour to figure out that one. Now, when I have to park at the airport, I write on a piece of paper the floor, the aisle number, and the section so I can find it when I come back. In a parking lot in a mall, I will look for a marking or where it is in relationship to the storefront.

Children

The most precious gift that anyone can be blessed within their lives is the privilege of having a child. They make your house a home.

From the moment you hear the first cry up until they leave your home to start their own new life, and everything in between, is a blessing, and the memories will last a lifetime. Plus, even when they do leave the nest, it's wonderful to see how all the years of love, sacrifice, and teaching have paid off. It's very rewarding as a parent to sit back and watch.

I know that a lot of couples who do not have children for one reason or another, and a few who admitted to me personally that they truly would have liked the opportunity to raise a child of their own because they have witnessed families raising a child and felt a little envious or saddened that they could not experience the fulfilment of a family. The majority said that was what was missing in their life.

Then there are those who, although they could not have their own child, went a different route, and that would be via adoption. That is a lot of hard work with setbacks, and it requires patience and of course a lot of money because it is an expensive process. But in the long run, it is a small price to pay for a lifetime of love and laughter with their new addition. On top of that, they have given a child a chance to grow in a loving environment where their dreams are endless. It sure beats being in foster care, not that there is anything wrong with foster care, except that being adopted is more stable and with a loving family.

I am humbled by the sacrifice that parents make to raise a family, and all with unconditional love. Parents, give yourselves a pat on the back for a job well done.

I would like to think I am in the group that had the privilege of raising a child—and in my case, it was raising four rug rats. They still mean so much to me, and even to this day, I cherish the phone calls and the handmade birthday greetings that I receive. Don't get me wrong; there were times when the waters were not always calm. There were issues on the home front that had to be dealt with and, to be very honest, were not dealt with properly at times, and for that I say to my children, Jason, Nicholas, Andrew, and Jennifer, that I am sincerely sorry. It was not for a lack of trying because everything my children did, I was included in. That meant being a coach, tutor, therapist, personal driver, doctor, and teacher.

Thanks to them, I also became a Boy Scout master while living in Bolton, was an actor who portrayed Judas the apostle in the presentation of the Last Supper at the church while living in Woodbridge, and was elected to the parent council at my daughter's elementary school while residing in Etobicoke. These are just a few of what my children helped me achieve as a parent. Children inspire you to be a better person, step out of the box, and try new things. My children have taught me so much, so I wonder who benefited the most? They show us the simple things in life are free. They have no prejudice, no competition, no racism, and no hatred. They are too busy simply being kids, and maybe we should follow what our children are showing us, which is "Let's play and grow together, no matter who we are. No rich, no poor, no black and no white. We are all the same."

Having said all that, like most parents, there are firsts that happen. The majority are good, and a few are not so good. The following are firsts in my family that I have put together based on personal experience. I am sure most parents have a similar list. The list may be long, but let's not forget that I have four children, and as we all know, every child is different.

First Year

Poop

Smile

Laugh

Fall

Cut

Step

Hug

Walk (baby steps)

School

First day, kindergarten

First day, high school

First day, college/university

Concert

School trip

Report card

Interview

Picture

Graduation

Friend

Special Days

Christmas Day

Birthday

Father's/Mother's Day

Halloween

First Communion

Valentine's Day

Easter egg hunt

First pet

Medical

Doctor

Dentist

Emergency

Therapist

School nurse

Sports/Activities

Learning to skate and swim

Tee ball hit

Soccer goal

Bike

Car models

Lego

Card games

Growing Up

Car

Boyfriend/girlfriend

Police

Court

Drugs

Counselling

Army reserve

Family Outings

Cottage

Beach

Library

After Leaving the Nest

Marriage

New home

New car

Science centre	New job
Scout jamboree	Grandchildren
Camping	Celebrations all over again, only this time with more people
Trailer park	
Marshmallow roast	
Vacations	

There are so many memories that we have of our children that will last a lifetime. Even the not-so-good ones can be fun to go back to. Again, a sense of humour helps. You cannot put a price tag on these memories, and no amount of money could deprive me of the memories. I would not want to change any of the past. It just would not be the same. Thanks to Jason, Nicholas, Andrew, and Jennifer for my memories. I love you all the same now (no less and no more) as I did when you first entered my world.

Climate Change

Why is it taking so long for the world to acknowledge and accept the fact that climate change is a reality and that if nothing is done relatively soon, there will be no time to fix it—if it is not too late already?

I wish the political leaders of the world would get their heads out of the sand or out of their asses, to put it bluntly, and realize that climate change is now.

The pollutant capitals of the world—and you know who you are—should be held accountable for what is happening. They say that climate change is not real, and even though the science is proving otherwise on a daily basis, the truth is denied. Unfortunately, it comes down to the same obvious bottom line. When power, money, and greed are involved, anything that gets in the way of those three selfish words will ultimately be ignored, denied, and frowned upon.

Personally speaking, although I am not the sharpest tool in the shed, I am aware of what is happening to the planet. All I have to do is listen to the experts or watch what is happening around the world.

Wildfires that cannot be contained. Hurricanes and tornadoes becoming more frequent with catastrophic damage. Floods and mudslides destroying homes. The melting of glaciers because of the rising temperature, which is ultimately affecting our marine life environment. I could go on, but I think that my point is made. Honestly, I will not be around when the shit hits the fan, but I fear and worry that my children and grandchildren will pay dearly for what has been going on for decades, and it is increasing at such a rapid speed that it will be too late for them.

It starts with us by means of not only speaking up verbally but also taking action. Let us do our part to help climate change. One person can start doing the right thing, and the steps are so simple. If I can figure it out, then everyone can figure it out.

On an individual basis, let us try to do what is suggested that we do:

1. Speak up
2. Power your home with renewable energy
3. Weatherize your home
4. Invest in energy-efficient appliances
5. Reduce water waste
6. Actually eat the food you buy
7. Buy better light bulbs
8. Recycle

On a business basis, the following are the biggest causes of climate change:

1. Burning coal, oil, and gas, which produces carbon dioxide and nitrous oxide
2. Deforestation
3. Increasing livestock farming
4. Fertilizers containing nitrogen, which produce nitrous oxide emissions
5. Fluorinated cases are emitted from equipment and products that use gasses

In short, human activity is the main cause of climate change. People burn fossil fuels and convert lands from forests to agriculture ... burning fossil fuels produces carbon dioxide, a greenhouse gas. It is called greenhouse gas because it produces a greenhouse effect.

I read that while searching on Canada.ca website under a section stating the Causes of climate change, modified 2019-03-28 because as I mentioned earlier, I am not the sharpest tool in the shed, especially when it comes to science. All I know is that if we as a whole don't act now, I am afraid that it will have a devastating impact for future generations. That means my grandchildren and their children will be in for a lifetime of struggle to survive, but just as important, they will not be able to see the beauty of nature that I have seen, as many species of wildlife will be reduced in number or extinct. That is a reality.

Here is some food for thought: Why are we so gung-ho on space exploration to Mars? We should be investing right here on Earth to fix the issues caused by humans before it is too late. To me, it is a mission that is telling me that now that Earth is being destroyed, it is time to screw up another planet, starting with Mars. It is mind-boggling.

Commercials

Is it just me, or are there more commercials on TV now than there used to be a few years back? Also, are they not getting more ridiculous than ever to sell their product?

Case in point: for some silly reason other than being bored, I did a survey while watching some shows on TV. The first show, which was sixty minutes long, had twenty commercials ranging in length of thirty to ninety seconds each. It worked out to be approximately fifteen minutes in total length. The second show was similar to the first show regarding commercials. The third show was a thirty-minute show (paid programming, mind you), and although there was a lower percentage of commercials, it was a show about cleaning stuff for sale. Talk about irony. I will admit that the show was on at 4:00 in the morning, and who in their right mind watches a program about cleaning stuff that early in the day? I said "in their right mind," didn't I? I know what you are thinking.

Now, about the commercials. I will not mention them by name due to legality issues, but they are so stupid in order to grab your attention. Is that our society today? Do we have to resort to this kind of sales pitch in order to promote a product? The following are just a few examples.

Drugs. They spend twenty seconds telling you what it might help you with and forty seconds telling you how it may harm you. In short, the product may help you with an itch, but it may cause heart failure or possibly kill you. Explain the benefits to me please. I would love to hear why this product is being sold.

Insurance. They show scenarios of really silly accidents that happen (not in reality would these occur), and they state that it's easy to file a claim and get everything back to normal. If nothing else, these commercials give ideas to certain deranged individuals who may try to do these acts in order to start a claim. Whatever happened to normal and serious ads regarding insurance? And to those people watching, be advised of the small print, because in there you will find that insurance companies have certain policies, rules, and loopholes to cover their derrières, which means they may not help you in time of need.

Lottery commercials. These have to be right near the top of my not-to-do list because they are the corniest on TV. If anything, I have a habit of flipping the channel and hoping that when I flip back, the commercial is over.

Donation ads. There are far too many of these, and I have never even heard of some of the organizations. I heard that the majority of the money collected goes to pay the people who are promoting the organization, which means very little actually goes to help those in need. My suggestion is to donate locally to a charity you know, or better yet, do what I have done, which is volunteer. I have found volunteering to be extremely rewarding, and you know where your hard-earned time and money goes first-hand.

The only way commercials can be ignored is if you turn off the boob tube and do something else, like spending quality time with your children or significant other, pick up a book and read, or maybe, just maybe, go outside and enjoy some fresh air and an activity like golf or gardening.

Maybe that's what the commercials are trying to tell us. I am beginning to listen and watch less TV these days. Somewhere else in my book, I mention things happen for a reason, and this adds to that list.

Death (Why Worry?)

As others have done, and some still do on a regular basis, I used to think about the inevitable, which is death. I guess it's natural to think such a morbid thought every once in a while, when in everyday life, it seems to be all around us. All you have to do is listen to the radio while driving, and there seems to be a vehicle crash causing serious injury or death somewhere that you have heard of, and listen and wonder, *Could that happen to me? Am I next?*

You could be sitting at home, relaxing with a coffee or tea (I don't drink any beer or liquor), and watching the news, and you hear about a house fire that has claimed a life or two. You wonder, "Do I have to worry about my own house being safe?" Even while enjoying a barbecue in your backyard or a picnic in the park, it may cross your mind: "Am I safe from a drive-by shooting if it should happen?"

Your own personal health comes into question, especially if you pay too much attention to all the hype about what is good for you, what is bad for you, and medicines that are supposed to help you with such simple issues like pimples (zits) or skin rash but have side effects that could be so severe as to cause death. If you don't believe that, just listen to the commercials on the US networks. There is twenty seconds about how this pill could help you and then forty seconds about how it could hurt or kill you.

It's no wonder people get paranoid worrying about death. It's drilled into our heads, thanks mainly to the media. Or should I say, the media doesn't help. Well, let me tell you that I am over that hump, and whatever happens will happen. It doesn't matter how much preparation you do, how many precautionary measures you take, how many studies you read about the healthy foods, or how many safety stuff in a car there is. When your time is up, your time is up. To me, that means if I want to put a slab of butter on a slice of bread instead of a spot, I'm going to do it without hesitation. If I want to have an extra slice of pizza with pepperoni and sausage, I'm going to go for it. If I want an extra handful of potato chips, you're darn right I am going to indulge. I don't drink or smoke, so there is no need to go there.

To sum it up, after a very peaceful sleep, I have no problem leaving my house, going to my favourite fast food outlet, ordering my bagel with butter and a double-double coffee, getting back in my car, driving to a local park, sitting outside, and enjoying some quality time with Mother Nature with absolutely no worries about what could possibly happen. Chances are nothing will happen. I think there is a high percentage of something happening, if you think about it. So why worry?

I have mentioned before that life is too short and that it is a beautiful privilege to enjoy life. So, sit back, relax, and enjoy the brief time you have. When it's over, you can't go back to see and do what you didn't do because you were too focused on something you can't control. I know I am. It took me long enough to figure that out. But you know what? When it is my time to go, I will be going with a smile on my face, and just as Frank Sinatra said, "I did it my way!"

Did What I Had to Do

Over the years, we all make mistakes, make questionable decisions, or bend rules a bit. I have done my best to teach my children that honesty is always the best policy, which also means leading by example. Unfortunately, there is a little bit of guilt within me, and I have decided to get the not-so-honest acts of necessity off my chest.

When I say not-so-honest acts, I mean at the age of fourteen, I was on my own for the most part, going to high school and working three jobs to provide for myself the necessities: food, clothing, and a roof over my head. A favourite pastime of mine was playing pool at a local pool hall around the corner from my high school and downtown at a billiard establishment near one of my jobs at the Bay Dundas bus terminal. As time went by, people noticed my style and asked if they could play a game with me. I quickly learned that there was money to be made here, so I turned the tables on them and played poorly for a couple of games. When the stakes were raised, that was when my game went up, and I normally came home with extra cash in my pockets. The term *hustler* comes to mind. It could also be called an act of deceit or an act of dishonesty, but I did what I had to do to survive.

The scenario in high school was work hard, do your best during the semesters, and be rewarded with a grade that would exempt you from writing a final exam in any subject that you did well in. I considered myself to be a good student who was there to learn, and therefore I was extremely fortunate not to have to write many final exams, with mathematics being my favourite subject during my four years. That subject seemed to be kryptonite for a lot of students, so along with science, geography, history, and even English, a scheme was devised and proposed to me that I write the final exams for students seeking help. It was actually pretty easy to do. On the day of the exam, the student seeking my help and I would walk into the cafeteria to find out where the exam was being written, along with who was the teacher presiding over the exam. If there was a teacher present at the exam who knew who I was, then I would simply walk out, and the student in need was on his own. If not, then the student in need would walk out, wait outside the school for me after I finished his exam, hand over some money, and shake my hand, and we would carry on in different directions. There was pretty good money to be made back then. Depending on the exam, the amounts would vary from twenty-five to fifty dollars per exam, and I cashed in, especially on math. All I had to do was change my writing style a bit and do it as fast as I could to get out of the cafeteria. Again, I did what I had to do to survive, although this was a huge act of dishonesty and trust that has played heavy on my mind, especially when teaching my children that honesty is always the best policy. Never mind that in the pool hall, not only could I have been hustled, but I also could have been beaten up if an unsuspecting person found out my game plan. The high school one could have been worse because I could have been expelled from school. I was lucky on both counts, so I guess somebody was looking out for me. Thank you to that person.

Diehard Leaf Fan (No More!)

After all the years of watching the blue and white and hoping—no, praying—that this may be the year that they will bring the cup home, I will make the following announcement: "I have fallen off the bandwagon. And I will add *forever.*

I mean, how much more can one go through with the once pride of Toronto (also known as Canada's team), up to and including their last Stanley Cup, which was May 2, 1967?

As a young kid who lived and breathed blue and white, and even while playing street hockey with friends, I always imagined that I was a Maple Leaf. Like most kids, I dreamed of playing for the Leafs when we grew up. I remember watching them Saturday nights and the occasional Wednesday night alongside my dad. We listened to the play-by-play of Foster Hewitt. Priceless.

Back in the fall of 1969, I had the opportunity to have a few tips from a legend of the Leafs, Johnny Bower, one of the all-time greats. As a goaltender, I was in awe when he approached me while at practice at Maple Leaf Gardens one day. He skated with me and gave me some valuable tips, but the most important piece of information he shared with me was not used on the ice but off the ice, and it went something like this: "Never lose the desire to play the game, and remember it is a game. Therefore, have fun playing." Those are words of wisdom that I use today. Later that year, I broke my kneecap, and all dreams and aspirations of playing in the big league disappeared. Truthfully, although I had a huge heart and desire to play, there was a lack of size, and I have to admit that my skill level would have prevented me from going much further. So, after all is said and done, I played with friends, or played a little shinny when the opportunity arose, or rented myself out when a goaltender was needed at various rinks over the years. Extra money was always welcome, but I always remembered to have fun. Thanks, Johnny.

Back to the Leafs. Every year is the same. They tell us that they are in a rebuilding mode. With the exception of a few years, they are almost always in a rebuilding mode. And when they are not in a rebuilding mode, they always fall apart in the playoffs. On top of that, it seems they can't even make it past the first round. Now, let's add salt to the wound. I remember back on May 13, 2013, when the Leafs blew a 4–1 lead midway in the third period and lost to Boston in game seven of a first-round match. Pathetic. With the money these players make, one would think they could do better. Maybe the pay should be revised to suit their downfall in the playoffs. After all, it's about ego and money, like most sports.

I will say that the Leafs must be the best golfers of all NHL. After all, they are most always the first team to exit and therefore spend more time on the golf course. Even then, they probably can't win anything.

So, to conclude my venting of the blue and white, after decades of promise and hope only to be met with agonizing pain, frustration, and dejection, I will now burn my Maple Leafs jersey in effigy.

Fun estimate, and by the way, estimating is my bread and butter so to speak: Since May 2,1967, up to and including February 2, 2022, the Leafs have not won the Stanley Cup for approximately 54.7 years, or 657.1 months, or 2,857.1 weeks, or 20,000 days, or 480,000 hours, or 28,800,000 minutes, or 1,728,000,000 seconds. I may be off a bit with my math, but you get the picture. With this kind of time on my hands, I think that I have to get a life, or at least a new hobby.

Every Day's a Good Day

Although the title looks like a plug for my first book, it's not, but I guess it's too late to get out of that little guilt trip. There is no sense in trying, so I will simply state why the saying is back. It is here because it's worth mentioning that life is so short, and we are all here on borrowed time. Unfortunately, it can be snatched away without any warning with no concern of age, gender, race, or religion.

We all should stop complaining about life and simply embrace our time here together. I mean, why can we not just tear down the walls of hatred between us? We are privileged to be here and enjoy life to its fullest. I enjoy life with words of happiness, inspiration, humbleness, and thanks, along with actions of helpfulness and giving. It is quite a simple philosophy, but then again, I am no different than other people. I am not better than anyone, nor am I less worthy than anyone. We are all created equal with the same reason for being here. Enjoy life and what it has to offer. Hell, at my age, when I wake up, I know it's going to be a good day. It's another day to share words, feelings, and happy moments with the ones I love. If we all tried that, it would be a much happier place.

Excuses

Have you ever listened to how people can come up with lame and unrealistic excuses for their misfortunes in everyday living? I mean, some of the excuses are so silly, it's impossible to listen to the person saying the excuse with a straight face and have an understanding point of view. It's also insulting that we are expected to believe them.

The following are just a few of the lame excuses for lack of thinking before doing or speaking of it after the fact. Just admit that you made a mistake or didn't think this could happen. We are human, and we all make mistakes at times—young and old, especially males.

A) Being late for an appointment

- The directions to get here were not clear.
- My bus was later than usual, which meant I missed my connection.
- The road conditions made me go slower (snow/ice/wind/rain).
- The cars in front of me were going too slow.
- There were too many red lights.
- I had to follow a lengthy detour.
- I needed gas.
- I needed my coffee from Tim's, and the drive-through was slow.

Solution: Leave a few minutes earlier, if it is that important. As for getting lost because directions were bad, I can't buy that because most cars and phones have GPS now. If not, look before you leave.

B) Not getting homework done on time

-   My dog ate my homework (an oldie but a good one).
-   Supper took longer, and I had to do dishes.
-   I had to take out the garbage.
-   My brother was making too much noise.
-   My favourite show was on TV.

Solution: Organize your time management and ask for parental help to alleviate the distractions.

C) Car repairs

-   I don't have the money to fix the problem.
-   I did not have the time to have it looked at.
-   I lost my mechanics phone number.

Solution: Proper maintenance helps lower big repair costs. Remember the commercial a long time ago, when the mechanic is looking at the engine and says, "You can pay me now or pay me later"?

D) Athletes (this category is endless, but here are just a few for examples)

Football, missed field goal: The wind blew the ball wide of the uprights.

Baseball, hit batter: The pitcher says the ball slipped out of his hand.

Hockey, missed an empty net: Looks at and blames his stick, as if it was the stick's fault.

Basketball, a slam-dunk is missed: Blames the net, or looks silly while trying to figure out why he missed.

Soccer, acting out being hurt on the field: Way overdone, but I heard it is also practiced in order to perfect it during the game.

Golf: The sound of change rattling in a fan's pocket threw off my concentration. The same is said for a sneeze, cough, or any body movement that may be in the golfer's view, no matter how far away the person is.

Tennis, missing a ball: Looks at the racket as if here is a hole in it. Noise from crowd is distracting: Have you ever listened to some of the players? They make sounds like they are having an orgasm, giving birth, or trying to have a bowel movement.

Solution: Concentrate and practice on your profession. Things happen. Just deal with it.

FYI, any person younger than me should not try to give me an excuse for anything for the following reason: I was young once and have experienced all the excuses just listed. I have heard them all and maybe even used a few myself.

False Teeth

Unfortunately, playing hockey takes a toll on one's body in one way or the other. Whether they be a few broken bones, torn muscles, scars from numerous cuts, bruising from being punished by opposing players, and sad to say concussions, injuries are more imminent these days. My body is no different. The only difference now is that I have parts that hurt where I didn't even know I had parts.

Like many others, I lost all of my upper set of teeth before I turned twenty-five thanks to a horizontal swing of a hockey stick by an irate hockey player who thought that he was playing baseball and that my mouth was the ball. It was a home run swing, to say the least. Back then, there was no choice but take out what was left of my teeth sticking out, and as they say, the rest is history.

Now, I have a full upper and partial lower. (Who knows how long that is going to last, considering the history?) Over the years, there have been a few adventures with them because they do have to come out on occasion for cleaning and maintenance. I will mention two stories that are funny now, though they were not funny back then.

I was a little behind for a meeting on my way to the office in Oakville, and my routine was to grab something to snack on while driving. This time it happened to be an apple. Without thinking (what else is new), I bit into this apple, and guess what? Snap, crackle, and pop (like the cereal), the denture was in two pieces. I had to fulfill my obligations at work but left right after my last words to have it glued back together at my dentist.

That denture lasted over forty years. It was good workmanship but was long overdue to be retired.

My son Andrew, around seven years of age at the time, was mad at me for grounding him, and because he had a history of getting back at me, this story is no surprise at all, but at the time it was not funny. First thing in the morning, again I was rushing to go to an early meeting. I discovered the dentures were not in the container in the bathroom where I had left them the night before to clean them. I had no choice but to leave without them, knowing full well that Andrew had something to do with it, especially when he looked at me and casually said, "Don't forget to smile at the meeting." At night when I got home, he pulled them out from the couch, looked at me with beady eyes, and sarcastically said, "Look at what I found."

There are others!

At least with COVID, when my mouth hurts, I can alleviate the irritation by removing the upper or lower dentures because no one will know when the mask is on. I just have to remember not to talk too much. Hey, I'm trying to find a positive during the pandemic.

The moral of the story is simple: Take proper care of your teeth.

Forgotten Art

This could be seen coming as soon as the first computer evolved back in what is known to kids as the prehistoric age.

Ever since the evolution of computer technology to what it has become today—and heaven forbid, what it will be like in the formidable future—it's really no wonder that handwriting will soon be just a memory. You really cannot blame the youth of today because that is how they are taught, and not just while in school but also what is shown to them by means of the media, stores, and the internet. Regardless of what is happening, I truly hope that writing is not going to be a forgotten art.

There is nothing more satisfying to me than when I receive a birthday card with a personal message written inside, or a letter that was actually mailed and not emailed or texted. I enjoy reading the letter because you can tell that effort has been put into the writing. I honestly savour the moment when a letter arrives. There is also a routine that I follow in order to get the quality time with the letter. A fresh cup of coffee is made, followed by a walk to a seat nearby, where I mentally block out any surrounding distractions before I open the envelope. The effort that is put into this little gem is probably too much work for some. I mean, you first have to grab a pen and paper, write what you want to say, put the letter into an envelope, put the address on the envelope, put your return address on the envelope, put a stamp on the envelope (Are you tired yet?), lick the envelope so it is sealed, and then physically put the envelope in the mailbox for it to be mailed. (Now you're tired, right?) It is a lot of work, but I greatly appreciate it. I know that emailing can be faster, but in all honestly, I get more satisfaction out of sitting down with a handwritten letter. You can actually understand the feelings of the person who wrote the letter at the time of writing.

The same goes for birthdays. Nothing beats the feeling one gets when opening a birthday card with a personal, handwritten message for your special day.

Over the years, I have accumulated letters, birthday and Christmas cards, pictures, and notes that my children gave me when they were growing up, including handmade birthday cards. To this day, I still get a fuzzy, loving feeling when I pull them out every once in a while, to take a nostalgic look at the past. And do you know what? The feeling I get is similar to when I first saw them. Priceless.

I hope that handwriting is not going to disappear any time soon because I think it is a vital tool that is beneficial to our everyday life. I may be getting old, but I will share one piece of information that hopefully will stop and make you think about what I have mentioned. Simply put, paper can be forever, whereas emails get deleted, computers crash, and phones get stolen.

Golf (Mis)adventures

Although I have been playing golf for quite a few years now, I have discovered one very notable summary. Instead of getting better with age, I am getting worse. The saying goes that people are like a fine bottle of wine: the older one gets, the better they get. Well, let me make this very clear that there are exceptions to every rule, and in this case, I am the perfect example in the game of golf.

I talked to my regular group of golfers to help me with the following, and they gladly volunteered to help me. According to them, it was easy because there are so many to mention, even in such a short period of time playing. The following misadventures were compiled by our regular foursome. I also noticed that I had the highest percentage of miscues. I would say it would be embarrassing for most, but like I have mentioned a few times, although I may not be a good golfer, I am gifted with a pretty good sense of humour. Along with me are Kiran, Nam, and Yasu to make up our foursome. Thank goodness for their patience and sense of humour.

We all have our sayings, and they are as follows.

Yasu: *"Let's get this over with."*

Kiran: *"It's doable."*

Nam: *"Chip and putt."*

Terry: *"Too far to par."*

Now for the (mis)adventures.

Our friend Kwan was at Dentonia Park. One hole was parallel with Victoria Park. He made three consecutive drives onto the road. I think he hit one car.

At Cardinal Golf Course, I hit a tree, and the ball went left onto another green, where a foursome was putting. I walked nonchalantly around the group, picked up my ball, apologized, and came back. They were not very receptive when I arrived to get my ball.

Yasu hit a ball and shanked it. It went left through my legs and hit our friend Massimo on the thumb. Massimo had trouble working after that for a bit. He still owes me for the round because he left early to take care of his hand.

I inadvertently took the wrong golf cart on a hole. It left the others scratching their heads.

I hit a Canada goose, hit one seagull in flight, and hit and flipped a turtle who was in a sand trap.

I went to the wrong golf course. I went to Cardinal, but it was supposed to be Glen Eagle.

Nam nailed a Canada goose.

Yasu has a knack for finding turtles.

Yasu looked for balls in a marsh area. He came back with balls, but he left his ball retriever in the marsh.

Yasu hit a ball through a cart and just missed two golfers sitting in the cart. The ball sailed over the golfers' heads and just under the roof of the cart.

I hit a ball that hit a tree and came back. I had to jump out of the way. My second shot was maybe one hundred yards. Then my third shot was around 150 yards.

I hit the wrong ball on the fairway. Even with initials, I still hit the wrong ball.

While playing a round with a co-worker and a couple of co-op students, I was going to pick up both mine and a co-op student's ball at the same time (shotgun style). Both balls were close to a marsh, and I assumed that there was not much water. I tiptoed, and just as I went to pick up the ball, I fell right into the marsh up to my butt. When I put both arms back to support myself to get up, I got a cramp in one of my legs. Without thinking of my predicament, when I changed positions with my arms, I fell backwards and right in. When I got up, I was soaked from the tips of my shoes up to my neck. I still played the rest of the round (not thinking there were another eight or nine holes to go). The other three stayed away from me. It might have been the odour of the clothes or the noise of my shoes walking with that squishing sound.

At a company tournament, I was wearing a kilt[1] (being part Scottish, I took the challenge of wearing the Gordon Kilt; check the book cover). While talking and walking towards the first hole at 7:00 a.m., I stepped on a railway tie and slipped with both feet in the air, and my kilt waved like Marilyn Monroe's pose on the infamous New York City street vent. The only difference was my kilt was facing upwards.

Note: railway ties are coated with creosote. Very slippery when wet.

Not very often do I hit a decent shot off a tee, especially a par three, but this time I did. When I stepped to my right a couple of steps, I inadvertently tripped over the block, fell, and rolled down the hill. I had a bruise for

---

[1] Wearing a kilt alleviates the need to find a place to go tinkle while playing a round of golf. No need to find a Johnny on the spot, and no need to hide in the bushes while doing your thing. Just stand to the side of the green or the side of the putting green and do your thing. Real golfers know what I am talking about.

weeks on my right side because I had two golf balls in my pocket. That hurts.

The golf bag fell off the golf cart because it was not strapped in. The noise of the bag when it hit the pavement took Nam off guard, and as he went to step onto the sidewalk, he tripped and fell, scraping his hand and leg and injuring his chest a bit. Although it affected his game a bit, I still could not beat him.

I have Scottish blood in me, and it has come into play while at the golf course. Having said that, a couple of years ago, my walking cart straps that secure the bag to the cart either fell off, broke off, or disappeared after the last game of the previous year. Being true to form and not wanting to buy a new cart, the solution seemed to be a no-brainer, and that was to get a piece of rope, some duct tape, or big elastic bands and tie/tape the bag to the cart. Unfortunately, none have worked that well. I guess it's time to invest in a new one so I don't have to pick up my bag, which falls off at least once every round when walking the course.

Let me also clear up a myth about the Scottish people, and that is we are not cheap but rather are frugal.

August 2, 2021, was the first time in my life golfing that I used the same ball from the first tee of the first hole to the last putt on the eighteenth hole. I never lost a ball. The ball has been retired and put in a safe place. There is a first for everything, I guess, and it is probably the last time.

Yasu, my best friend of over fifty years, and I have to check with each other before every round because we have been known to wear the same coloured golf shirts and even the same coloured pants. To make sure it doesn't happen again, I have learned to put an alternative coloured outfit in the car just in case.

While playing a round at Centennial Golf Course a few years back, we came across a snake slithering across the green. We decided to remove the snake slowly and carefully, with a golf club, put him into the nearby bush.

This one is unique. How about hitting a fairway shot and have it be a worm killer? You know, right at grass level. Well, I hit one of those shots which collided with my partners ball, which coincidentally was about twenty feet in front of mine and sent both balls up in the air and when they landed both were approximately five yards from a shallow stream which crossed the fairway. That would have been a first, even for me. You know, hit 1 ball and put 2 balls in the water at the same time.

Last but not least, it is hard to believe, but I had not even played a game last year, and I had already lost three balls. Let me explain. The opportunity came when I purchased a bag of mature balls like I do at the beginning of every golf season. Mature golf balls are balls that have already seen the golf course and been lost by others, scooped up, cleaned up, repackaged, and resold at a cheaper price. They're good for those who lose balls quite frequently (like me). Well, the bag was put in the back of my car, and after a few weeks of putting other things in and pulling things out, the bag unravelled, eventually allowing balls to escape. When I opened the back hatch and lifted up the door, six balls fell out and rolled in every direction in the parking lot. I managed to grab three, while one went under a parked truck, and the other two went down the storm drain. Even without playing, my balls get lost in the water. Some things never change.

Goodbye

Goodbye is a noun meaning

1) A concluding remark or gesture at parting—often used interjectionally
2) A taking of leave

Goodbye is also short for "God be with you."

Goodbye is a rather short word in length but is so long in meaning. It can be endless if you think about it. Saying goodbye could have a long-lasting effect to not only the person you say it to but also to yourself. I can't speak for everyone, but after the goodbye, I always wonder when I will have the opportunity to converse again with this person. That is especially true when talking to someone not so close, where you have to go a fair distance to visit. That trip could be across the street, across the city, across the country, or across the ocean. Let me give you a couple of examples.

My daughter, Jennifer, lives in Toronto and has a busy life, but she always makes time to phone or text to see how I am doing, and I will do the same when I need a pick-me-up or because I am thinking of her at the moment. Every conversation is heartfelt and appreciated, and it always puts a smile on my face and a warm feeling in my heart. The goodbyes plus the additional "I love you" really makes my day better no matter what is going on. The same can be said for my sons Nicholas, Jason (he should call me more often, though), and Andrew.

In the fall of 2016, I reached out to Keith Mack (a retired co-worker who moved back to the UK to enjoy life after his illustrious career in construction) and made arrangements to spend a few days with him and his wife, Julia, before heading onwards towards my first ever safari to Africa. It went by so fast, but I was very grateful to have spent the time with them catching up, sharing stories, and laughing. They are a beautiful couple, and to this day, they still keep in touch. The goodbyes and hugs were priceless and are etched in my mind forever. You see, Keith was well liked and respected within our company. Every now and then, his name is brought up, and a happy time is reborn again. That is why I fought back tears when I left Keith and Julia.

To be quite honest, I don't cry. In fact, I don't ever shed tears, regardless of the situation, whether it be a happy time (wedding, birthday) or a not-so-happy time (death, job loss, accident). In fact, the last time I cried was at my mother's funeral in October 1964. Less than two months after my twelfth birthday, my mother passed away of cancer. The reason for my outburst at the service was that reality had finally set in that I was never going to see her again, not even to say goodbye. That still haunts me to this day. That is why whenever I do say goodbye, there is more feeling, love, or concern put into the word than the just the literal meaning of the word.

That is why a big test is going to come when I, like Keith, finally give up my estimating career to enjoy my last chapter of life with no stress. I will enjoy those close to me on a more frequent basis. The reason I say this is because where I work, the people are more like family, not co-workers. Over the years, we have shared experiences just like a real family. There are too many to write, and I would be here for quite a while if I tried to mention them all. In short, I have been blessed to be with such wonderful, hard-working professionals who have helped me one way or another while I have had the pleasure of being here at Hardrock, Hardwall, Alpine, and Dell-Core. It is a first-class organization that I will miss greatly. So, when that time comes (hopefully not for a little while yet, but you never know), if I don't shed a few tears after those goodbyes, it will be nothing short of a miracle.

Growing Old (Not so Gracefully)

It seems the older we get, the more we forget. I am sharing some of the senior moments I have personally had. I hope I am not alone in this category, but you have to laugh at the misadventures. Otherwise, you will go crazy. I hope you enjoy my misadventures.

-   When on the phone (hands free of course) and driving on highway, you pass the exit you were supposed to get off at, only to realize a little bit later you are now entering a different city.
-   Save and Save As on a computer. I got them reversed last week with eight pages of take-off numbers. Thank God I had already printed out the pages. I simply had to retype them.
-   Where are my glasses? Oh, they are on the top of my head.
-   With my left hand holding my backpack on my shoulder and holding two sets of drawings, I could not find the phone. I then struggled with my right hand to use the office phone to call my cell. When my phone rang, I discovered it was in my left hand.
-   Misplacing car keys, house keys, wallet, glasses, cups of coffee, and more.
-   Wearing two different socks. (if younger, it's a brain fart)
-   Wearing two different shoes. (also, if younger, it's a brain fart)
-   Forget to put on underpants.
-   I took my time to make a shopping list. When at the store, I noticed that I had forgotten the list at home.

- I forgot which entrance I entered at a large shopping mall so as I could exit the same which would have made it easier to find the car.
- I've gone to the wrong golf course waiting for my group. Meanwhile, they are waiting for me at a different course.
- It's hard to put socks on without hurting something.
- I go upstairs in the house and forget why I went upstairs in the first place.
- I forgot to take the cardboard off a frozen pizza before putting it in the microwave.
- I came to the office once and the golf course once with my shirts inside out and buttoned.
- I keep forgetting to pull up the zipper of my pants before I go outside.
- I left for a meeting at a job site or office meeting, only to forget that my dentures are still soaking in a container at home.
- I go to the store for the sole reason to buy something either as simple as a bag of milk or gas for the car, but when it is time to pay, wouldn't you know it, my wallet is still on the table at home. This is not a one-time event, either.
- I go to the washroom for a good movement, to put it in as nice words as I can, only to carry on with my day and finally notice that my wallet is no longer in my back pocket. While trying to figure out which spot I left it in my travels, I came to a conclusion that I should cancel my credit cards, debit card, and more to prevent any possible fraudulent activities. Then after I did all of the cancellations, guess what? I found my wallet. It slipped out of my back pocket when I sat on the toilet and was still there on the floor when I passed by the washroom. That was the first time.
- The second time, it was also in my office, but that time I drove back home thinking I had left it in the house only to find out it wasn't there. After that disappointment, I checked the McDonald's where I bought a coffee on my way to the office, with no luck there. So here I went again cancelling my cards, only to find that when I went back to the office, the cleaner had found it and left it

on the reception desk. Talk about feeling really embarrassed. Now, when I put it in my pants, I make sure the pocket is buttoned up, or when I wear my cargo pants, the wallet is in front, where the pockets have a flap and are quite deep. You can never be too sure.

- To get to the second floor at my office, there are twenty-two steps. I swear, that by the end of the day, it feels like there are twenty-five steps or more.

I will once again state what I have said before: thank goodness I have been blessed with a good sense of humour.

Hair Issues

This could possibly be a no-brainer, or in my case a no-hair-to-cover-my-brain, but nevertheless, I still have an issue with hair.

For one, why should I have to pay the same amount of money for cutting my hair, which consists of cutting hair so it's above the ears and cutting hair at the back of my neck, which no one sees anyway, as the next person, normally a lot younger than me, who has a head of hair that Godzilla would be proud of? It is not fair. I mean, I am only there about ten minutes to get the job done, and that includes trimming my eyebrows. There is nothing to cut on top. I wish there was a natural fertilizer to help my hair grow. You know, like the stuff that makes your grass long, thick, and green. In my case, it's short, thin, and grey.

The other issue is even with the little hair that I do have, why is it always out of place or sticking up like Alfalfa's? You know, Alfalfa from *Our Gang*. Maybe not. I think my hair has it in for me, trying to get payback for my lack of cutting it during my hippie days. The only thing I do like when I get a haircut is the pleasant conversations I have with the barber or hair stylist. They are very nice to talk to, and I have to admit I always leave with a smile on my face. I guess that I should not complain too much, as there is a senior's discount is worth noting.

Happen for a Reason

How many times have things happened with a negative perspective as you would have described it, only to find out that something positive comes out of it that you never would have thought that probably saved you time, or money, or aggravation later down the road?

I will share a few of these with you, with the worst at the time becoming the best outcome that I could have possibly asked for. If not discovered at the time, I might be in a different (negative) stage of my life, if here at all to talk about it.

1) Leaving the house in a hurry and forgetting some office work or drawings that I need (yeah, that happens from time to time) when I leave for the office first thing in the morning, only to realize about fifteen minutes later that I have to return home to collect the work. At first, I am frustrated, but upon my numerous returns, the following had to be done:
    a) Lock the door.
    b) Close the garage door.
    c) Turn off at least one light, possibly two.
    d) I had started an early morning watering of the grass and had to turn off the sprinkler; that would have been a small disaster ten hours later.
    e) Bring my lunch.
    f) Take out the bins on recycling day.
    g) Put my wallet in my pocket.

It's sad, but the above mentioned has happened more than once.

2) Going into the supermarket for a few items and then realizing when I get inside, I discover my list is not with me. Now I have to go back to the car and retrieve my list only to also realize my wallet is on the passenger seat (I just used it at the gas station), my keys to the car are also on the passenger seat, and obviously the door wasn't locked, so there was a chance that my car would not be there when I came out. Whoever stole the car would have cash for dinner plus my credit cards for more gas later.

3) Getting an illegal crosscheck to the back of my head while playing some hockey (shinny, as it goes by), followed by my face hitting glass and then smacking my head on the ice when I fell down. The combination of those three hits gave me what is commonly known as severe grade 4 concussion, which means knocked out and then followed by sporadic memory loss, headaches, balance issues (walking), and more. The symptoms were pretty severe for up to fourteen days and then thankfully deteriorated after that. Now the good part—and yes, there is a good part. A follow-up X-ray was taken after the swelling and cloudiness subsided, and it was discovered that there were two spots on my little brain. Although not too serious, they grow and put pressure on my brain, which is a concern because my headaches were getting worse in severity and lasting longer each time they occurred. That issue is a work in progress and is well under control with no worries. But without that knock on my noggin, I would have never known, which means the problem would have never been looked at, which means there could have been a different outcome due to the lack of priority in taking care of the problem. That could be life-changing, to say the least. So yes, there is a happy ending to this. I am sure everyone has a story to tell, but maybe not the silly ones I have done.

Hillbillies and Rednecks

The official definitions of hillbillies and rednecks are as follows.

> Hillbilly: a person from a backwoods area; 1881 first known use (Merriam-Webster's Dictionary)

> A person from the backwoods or remote mountain area (Free Dictionary)

> Redneck: A white member of the southern Rural Labouring Class; 1830 first known use (Merriam-Webster's Dictionary)

> A person regarded as having a provincial, conservative, often bigoted attitude (Free Dictionary)

I hate to be the bearer of bad news—or it could be good news to me—but both of these words have Celtic roots. Let me explain with definitions according to UK history.

Hillbillies and rednecks have their origins in Scottish roots. The origins are distinctly Scottish and Ulster-Scottish, and they date to the mass immigration of Scottish Lowland and Ulster Presbyterians to America during the 1700s.

The nickname *hillbilly* comes from Ulster. Ulster-Scottish settlers in the hill-country of Appalachia brought their traditions with them to the new world after William, prince of Orange, defeated the Catholic King James II at the Battle of Boyne, Ireland, in 1690.

The origin of *redneck* refers to supporters of the National Covenant and the Solemn League and Covenant, or Covenanters, largely lowland Presbyterians, many of whom would flee Scotland for Ulster (Northern Ireland) during persecutions by the British Crown. The Covenanters of 1638 and 1641 signed the documents that stated that Scotland desired Presbyterian form of church government and would not accept the Church of England as its official state church.

Many covenanters signed in their own blood and wore red pieces of cloth around their necks as distinctive insignia—hence the term *red neck*, which became slang for a Scottish dissenter.

That's my one and only history lesson that I will share with you. History was not my favourite subject in school, and I just barely passed the course. Considering that my father was born in Leith, Scotland, that makes me a Canadian with Scottish heritage, and I am quite proud of it.

To be honest, I had no idea that a redneck and a Scotsman could be affiliated in the same category. I should have realized it when I moved to Alliston, which is nicknamed as one of the redneck communities, that I would become a redneck, so to speak. Wait a minute—I thought in order to be a redneck, you had to have at least three distinctive qualities or items:

1) Pickup truck
2) Shirts with cut-off sleeves
3) False teeth

Having thought of what I just wrote, it has come to my attention that I have two out of the three qualities. So, if majority rules, I guess I could be classified as a redneck. But in all honesty, now that I know that it is also a Scotsman's quality, it's not so bad.

Idiots of a Lifetime

A few French fries short of a happy meal.

As smart as a box of rocks.

Not the brightest crayon in the box.

The lights are on, but no one's home.

A few bricks short of a load.

The engine's running, but no one is behind the wheel.

A couple yards short of a first down.

A wheel short of a road test.

Glasses are on, but eyes can't see.

A couple inches short of a par.

Not the sharpest tool in the shed.

A few pieces short of a completed puzzle.

A few letters short of an alphabet.

A few cents short of a dollar.

A few minutes short of an hour.

A sandwich short of a picnic.

A few cans short of a six-pack.

Half a bubble off plumb.

The elevator doesn't go up to the top.

There have been numerous times over the years where I have had discussions (some serious and some not so serious) regarding matters of politics, sports, health, construction, and cost consultants. Wait—the last one is a little too close to home and still gets my blood flowing when I have to deal with them on occasion. Don't get me wrong; they are a necessity in the industry and for the most part keep us subcontractors honest by not fabricating or escalating costs, especially on extras to contract. I do have the utmost respect for them, but I wish they would understand how things work from our point of view. I mean, it has gotten to the point where I have to spell out how I do my estimate and changes. We even have to attach a supplementary document detailing how we estimate the job, and they still have the audacity to question and disagree. It is very frustrating, to say the least. For those few, and others such as politicians, in-laws, and neighbours (I will not mention names so as not get myself in trouble), the following pejorative meaning is for many who are out there. I am sure you have people in the same category. Maybe you could share a few of them.

- Pejorative – meaning not very intelligent or of questionable mental capacity.

Immigration

There are two completely different directions I am going with immigration.

One part of me wants to see people from other parts of the world be allowed to come to Canada for a better way of life, because we have it pretty good here. I love the diversity we have with different nationalities. As a Canadian-born citizen, it's a very rewarding learning experience to know about other cultures. The world is a beautiful place, and to learn about the customs, culture, history, religion, and dress styles is priceless. I am humbled that they proudly share their own countries when they come here. I also believe we need these people. There is a shortage of highly skilled professionals, which includes any position from construction workers to doctors to engineers to scientists and everything in between.

Our country was built with immigrants who came here with nothing more than the shirts on their backs and the will to build better lives for themselves and their families. They asked for nothing except a chance to work and contribute to help our country's growth. For the most part, I believe in that to be true today, but here is my problem with that scenario. From what I read and see, we are being taken advantage of by those who come here to do nothing, contribute nothing more than sit at home, and collect welfare and free medical care. They get a free place to live and do nothing but complain about their way of life while here. And what's with the protests? Whenever something happens back in their country, why protest here? We cannot do much to resolve the issue. I wish I could help, but if you feel so strongly about what you are protesting about, then I suggest you go back home to resolve the issue and fight over there. You are here in Canada. This is your new home. You have been given a chance for a better way of life, so adjust to the better way of life. Plus, it should be mandatory to speak or be willing to learn to speak English or French. That's not asking much, is it? I mean, if I were to uproot my family and myself and move to a foreign country, I would abide by all laws, even though I may disagree with some of them, and I would do my utmost to learn the language by any means possible. I would do it out of for respect for my new home.

The majority of newcomers do that, but the number that simply want to come here and get a free ride is increasing. A little birdie told me that there are websites out there that show how to fast-track the requirements to get here—and not the legal way—plus how to scam the system before you get here. In layman's terms, "Show me how to get welfare when I get there." And guess who pays for it? You and me with our taxes, which keep going up. I am not racist by any means because my circle of friends is quite diverse. I love everyone and will give everyone a fair shake. But when you get here, please contribute to Canada's way of life. That means work and pay taxes. Do you hear that, Mr. Trudeau? Stop being a bleeding heart to everyone. Oh, I forgot—it's good for re-election, isn't it? That's something to think about.

Inspiration

There have been many times when things seem to be impossible to achieve, or there are thoughts that cross my mind as I believe there seems to be a curse or grudge against me to prevent me from reaching my goals, no matter how hard I try. To be quite honest, they are very frequent and can be overwhelming.

I have not shared my latest setback with anyone, and I will definitely keep it within me. When it gets to the point of feeling sad and a little depressing, I will look for some kind of uplifting news from the outside world for any kind of inspiration. I know I can talk to family or friends, but there is a chance they will feel a little under the weather after we talk, and I have no intention of putting anyone in my frame of mind.

That's when I look for inspiration from outside the box, and there are two inspirational stories that have been reflected on time and time again to help me get through some difficult times.

The first inspiration that I noticed a few years ago was Greta Thunberg of Sweden, an environmental activist who is internationally known for challenging world leaders to take immediate action for climate change mitigation. She has been doing this since 2018, when she was fifteen. Even despite being targeted by critics, she is still following through with her message in order to help save the planet.

Second, there is Captain Sir Tom Moore of the UK, who walked one hundred laps around his garden while the country was in lockdown during the COVID-19 pandemic. He single-handedly raised 32 million pounds, or approximately 44.3 million US dollars. The man was one hundred years old.

If those two stories are not inspirational enough for you, I don't know what is. There are hundreds, if not thousands, of stories of inspiration out there to help you get through any tough, challenging times in your life.

All you have to do is shut your mouth, open your eyes, open your ears, and most importantly never give up your hopes and dreams regarding what you want to do. Nothing is impossible if you have heart, determination, and a passion to succeed. I realized that a long time ago, although I do need reminders every once in a while. When I do, I always think of the two people I have mentioned.

I also have some inspirational quotes that I have come across over the years, and they help me get through tough times or cross the finish line. I would like to share some of them. They may or may not help you, but I can guarantee you there are other quotes out there that will inspire you.

> Perfection is not attainable, but if we chase perfection, we can achieve excellence. —Vince Lombardi

> If you look at what you have in life, you'll always have more. If you look at what you don't have in life, you'll never have enough. —Oprah Winfrey

> None of us is as smart as all of us. —Ken Blanchard

> When I stand before God at the end of my life, I would hope that I would not have a single bit of talent left and could say, I used everything you gave me. —Erma Bombeck

> What's money? A man is a success if he gets up on the morning and goes to bed at night and in between does what he wants to do. —Bob Dylan

There is no royal road to anything. One thing at a time, all things in succession. That which grows fast, withers as rapidly. That which grows slowly, endures. —Josiah Gilbert Holland

When everything seems to be going against the wind, remember that the airplane takes off against the wind, not with it. —Henry Ford

I would rather die of passion than of boredom. —Vincent Van Gogh

When I hear somebody sigh, "Life is hard," I am always tempted to ask, "Compared to what?" —Sydney Harris

When I was five years old, my mother always told me that happiness was the key to life. When I went to school, they asked me what I wanted to be when I grew up. I wrote down "happy." They told me I didn't understand the assignment, and I told them they didn't understand life. —John Lennon

We can easily forgive a child who is afraid of the dark; the real tragedy of life is when men are afraid of the light. —Plato

Life is 10% what happens to me and 90% of how I react to it. —Charles Swindall

To handle yourself, use your head; to handle others, use your heart. —Eleanor Roosevelt

Instead of Complaining

As human nature would have it, complaining is a way of life for many people, and some are not happy unless they complain about something on a regular basis. Why is that? Heck, there are times when I complain as well, although fewer and fewer as time goes on. Well, there is a little secret that I would like to share with you. Although it is extremely simple, it is quite effective. That secret is to think about the positive of your situation and not the negative. It works every time.

Here are a few scenarios that made me stop and think in a more positive manner and be less selfish.

When stuck on a highway behind an accident, I was worried about being late to watch a Leafs game and thought to myself, "Why me?" It's not often I can go to these events. But when I first heard and then saw the ambulance and fire truck arrive, I knew there was something more serious than a fender bender. At that moment, I was glad that neither my family nor I were not part of the accident. When I finally got to my seat at the game, the Leafs were already losing, so I really didn't miss anything anyway.

On more than one occasion, like other families who have children, there will probably be a trip or two to the emergency ward at the local hospital. On one of these trips, I thought, "Why is this taking so long? After all, this is my child who needs attention, plus I have other things to do." Then it came to me that I had just had a great conversation with my child, which was so rewarding. We talked and laughed our butts off.

The other example that really opened my eyes was the time it had been raining for hours, and our family plans were dampened (no pun intended). Coincidentally, while we were killing time, there happened to be a *National Geographic* documentary on the idiot box regarding drought in the world and the devastation that it can cause, particularly the conditions that people have to endure to survive—if they survive. This included no clean drinking water, no clean water to get washed, no water to grow food, and more. It's hard to imagine life without one of nature's gifts to the world. Without rain, there would be a struggle to survive. Now, when it rains, I sit back, enjoy the rain, and watch as the earth is cleansed a little.

As I have said before, life is too short to bitch and complain. Simply relax and enjoy every day as if it is your last, because one day it will be your last.

Journey to Peace

Sometimes in life, the road to happiness does not come easy for some. There are steep hills to climb, speed bumps and potholes to avoid, and blizzards to overcome. But all in all, it can be accomplished with hard work, perseverance, and the will to make it happen, and that means asking for help (swallowing your pride) or doing it without having help (losing your self-pity). And don't forget a little sacrifice.

Growing up on the streets of Toronto during my teen years forced me to either have the will to make a future for myself or go the other way: give up on the idea of a happy life, become oblivious, and survive on the streets. I decided that my will was more outspoken than my self-pity.

I put my foot down and worked hard while in school, and although it was only high school, I graduated with honours. Sacrifice was a big part of my road to success, which now (and even back then) has finally turned into peace. As an example, on graduation night I had to work because I was on my own and needed to work to provide for myself. That also meant no parties, no dances, no clubs, no social activities, and no playing outdoors with friends on weekends. The meaning of sacrifice was drilled into me at an early age. But at that early age, I learned structure, responsibility, personal banking, and more. You have no choice but to learn when there is no option. You can't learn that in school. Today, I hear about adults young and old with money problems, debt, and credit card overspending, and I often wonder why this is not taught in school. There is no shortcut to success, peace, and tranquillity. Not all of us are born with a silver spoon in our mouth. It's hard work, but the rewards are endless.

Along the way, I have asked for help (swallowed my pride), saved, and bought whatever I wanted for myself, by myself (I lost the self-pity). Sometimes it took longer. It's been a long journey, but these days, I am reaping the rewards of that hard work and sacrifice, and believe it or not, every day seems to be a little better than the day before. I truly look forward to whatever comes my way because I now feel at peace with myself and what I have been through and accomplished. It's a good feeling. I just wish others could see it that way and learn by example.

Joy to the World

Before I expand on this, you should know that there is more to the title than meets the eye, and I have personally sung the words either in my mind or out loud when alone and not feeling in a very good state of mind.

It could be because of a very long and stressful day, or a tragedy that I have heard from the media, or an event that has affected me personally, especially if family is involved.

"Joy to the World" is a song from the band Three Dog Night and was introduced sometime in 1975. The song has lyrics that really don't have any special theme, message, or story to me other than a "feel good in the moment" jingle that almost always picks me up.

The beginning of the song goes as follows:

> Jeremiah was a bullfrog,
> Was a good friend of mine
> I never understood a single word he said
> But I helped him a-drink his wine
> And he always had some mighty fine wine
> Joy to the world
> All the boys and girls now
> Joy to the fishes in the deep blue sea

It's best that you go online and listen to this little gem, because you will appreciate the entire song with the music a lot more than what my memory has scribbled above.

In today's world, where there are a lot of troubles to be aware of, from COVID-19 to wars, environment issues, world starvation, and everything in between, it's nice to stop for a moment, even if only for a moment, and smile at what we do have, which is our personal way of life, while others struggle just to survive on a daily basis.

As I have mentioned many times before, life is a privilege and can be taken away in a moment's notice. This little song of happiness brings me joy every time I think of it, and we all need a little bit of happiness in our daily living. The world is a beautiful place, and although this song is not much of an answer to fix our troubled world, it sure brings joy to my world. It has a touch of humour and is a reminder to enjoy the most important things around us.

Keepsakes

Over the years, one goes through so many happy times: birthdays, graduations, promotions, family additions, new house celebrations, marriage, anniversaries, retirement—the list is endless.

Unfortunately, along with the happy times come the not-so-happy times: disappointments, divorce, joblessness, accidents, health issues, death—sadly, this list is also endless.

I have had my share of both, so there is an accumulation of mementos to help keep me grounded regarding my circle of life.

There are things in my closet I bring out from time to time that to this day bring tears to my eyes and a little warmth to my heart. These include black-and-white pictures of my immediate family, which consisted of not just my mother and father but also my brothers George, Edward, and Henry and sisters Dorothy and Vera, all of whom have been gone for such a long time, to small gifts given to me for keepsakes, along with the trust to keep them in the family and, when the time comes, pass them on to my children in order to keep the tradition alive and the memories alive.

The following are some items in my possession.

1) A copy of the *Globe and Mail* newspaper days after the *Titanic* sank, dated April 18, 1912
2) A work gift to my father stating ten years of service from his workplace, dated October 13, 1942

3) Canadian Tire mini tape (1993)
4) Bowling tie clip.
5) Hohner six-sided harmonica (including the original box)
6) My mother's signed guest book after she passed away (1964).
7) My father's Dutch couple lawn ornament, which stood outside the family cottage in Wasaga Beach while I was in my teens
8) My sister Dorothy's young boy and dog lawn ornament, which stood outside her trailer in Port Perry (it stands outside my home now, and I am reassured every day when I come home that I am safe and still protected by my big sister)
9) Stamps used during wartime for food rationing
10) Eulogies I have given over the years for family and friends (I think of them at times when not feeling too happy)
11) My Bible my mother gave me while I attended Sunday school around nine years of age; it is in plain view every day in my home office
12) My sister Vera's accordion
13) My father's six-sided harmonica

There are others that I have not mentioned because they are buried in places I cannot remember, but one day I will come across them, and when I least expect it, those memories will be with me again, if only for a few moments, happy or sad.

It is so important to cherish those memories that were part of our life at one time or another. To me, it is more important to pass these cherished keepsakes on to my children and grandchildren to keep the memories alive. I wish there were more to share, but I will take quality over quantity anytime. Plus, I have now introduced my mementos (I hope), which will leave an impression for generations to come after I am gone.

A word of warning: it may be a good idea to list the items, whether cherished memories or materialistic items and anything in between, with names of whom you would like to give them to. There have been too many family squabbles over what people think they are entitled to. It will take more than a lawyer to sort out that mess.

Kryptonite

We all know about Superman and his superpowers, and I believe we all know the one and only weakness that he has: kryptonite, which is depicted as an alien mineral from Superman's home planet that has the property of depriving Superman of his powers. The real meaning of kryptonite is "something that can seriously weaken or harm a particular person or thing."

Believe it or not, we all have our kryptonite one way or another. I know I have a couple.

One of my biggest ones would be joining my friends for a round of golf. If there is anything to do with water nearby, I will find it. That could be in the means of a stream, a pond, a marsh, or a puddle. You name it, and my ball will find it. There are a couple of holes where I have been known to walk up to the water, toss an old ball in the water, and move on. Although on a couple of occasions, the ball has skipped across the water like a skipping stone and actually found its way back on the fairway.

To emphasize and prove that water is my kryptonite, just take a look at my golf misadventures for the ultimate proof. Or better yet, just ask anyone of whom I have had the pleasure to play with.

The following are a few categories and their corresponding kryptonite.

Subject	Kryptonite
Toronto Maple Leafs	First-round playoffs
Doug Ford	Opening his mouth on COVID
Novak Djokovic	Olympics
A lot of welfare recipients	Work
Non-vaccinated people	Needles (plus a little ignorance)

I am sure that you also have observed similar, but these are just a few of my pet peeves that get on my nerves. I am learning to ignore them one by one, starting with the Leafs.

Laughter

Laughter is just one word, but it has so much meaning. Can you imagine if we all dropped what we were doing and decided to laugh? And if we did it at the same time, what would that look like or sound like? On second thought, maybe that is not a good idea because we would probably be wearing a white jacket backwards and put in a padded room.

It sounds contradictory, but on a serious side for a moment, wouldn't it be enjoyable to spend our time with nothing but smiles on our face and laughing so hard that our belly hurts? It would be a nice hurt. Beats the hell out of anger, I tell you.

I am going to mention my nephew Marty because he has a laugh so contagious that if he could get a patent for it, he would be the richest man around. His laugh is that original and sincere.

Just by observation, watch a child, or a couple of children, playing. It is a sight of innocence, and it's heartfelt to hear the sound of laughter and the smiles they share. Without looking like a stalker, I always try to observe the smiles and sounds of laughter from children. I think we all can learn so much from someone so young. Try it; it can be addicting. But if not, at least it will put a smile on your face.

Lawnmowers

Over the years of house ownership, there have been many lawnmowers that have come and gone. It started with a push mower at the family cottage at Wasaga Beach back in the mid-1950s. I was too young to push it but watched my dad do it.

Our first home in Bradford, somewhere around 1978. That was where the gas lawnmower was introduced to me, and I found it strangely enjoyable being outside in the sun, walking around the yard, and cutting the grass (along with a few plants that should not have been cut). A conversation with a neighbour would almost be a regular thing on a Sunday afternoon. It wasn't work for me but rather a social outing. Good, neighbourly friendships would evolve from these outings. Who knew?

As time went by, there have been a few others, including one that came with the trailer I purchased up in Port Perry approximately a year after my separation. That was one of the best investments for my well-being at a time when I was going in circles trying to figure out what happened to my marriage of twenty-four years. Although it was a little overpriced, it truly helped me get going again, and believe it or not, cutting the grass was a positive outing because it was relaxing and created a chance to chat with neighbours. It was an old gas mower that you could not kill if you tried. Every fall I would put the mower, gas and all, underneath the trailer for winter storage, and every year in late spring when the park opened, the mower started on the first pull. Amazing!

I even had a lawnmower called the Flymo, which was a gas mower with no wheels. Its design was taken from a hovercraft, which meant it floated on air. All you had to do was push it, and away you go. It was easy. Unfortunately, it was too easy because I caught my son Andrew (about seven at the time) one afternoon cutting the grass in the backyard. I went out to thank him for helping, but more to let him now that he should not be doing it because it could be dangerous; his little foot could fit under the mower while the blades were spinning, which could cause a very serious injury. He said he was trying to be like his dad. It was flattering to say the least, but when I noticed the two empty cans of beer by the patio, I suddenly realized he had been watching me and took it upon himself to have a beer during yard work. Do you know how much trouble I could have been in if someone had noticed and called social services, or worse, if an accident took place, and Andrew needed medical attention, but at the ER, someone could smell beer on his breath? It would have been tough explaining that one. For the remainder of the day and night, I would not let Andrew out of my sight, just in case.

The past eight years at my home in Alliston, it has been back to the four-wheeled gas mower with a keyed start as well as the traditional pull cord start. Well, let me tell you, the keyed start does not function anymore, which leaves the pull cord. No matter how much I take care of this machine, it has given me major issues the past few years. In the fall after the last cut, I empty the gas tank, clean the filter, wipe the blades, and wipe the mower itself before putting it in the garage for hibernation, yet every spring with fresh gas, I cannot get it started. It is frustrating, to say the least. Instead of paying someone fifty dollars to get the mower up and running, last year I decided to go back to where it all started, and that meant buying a push lawnmower. No more gas mowers, no more electric mowers, no more buying gas and making a little mess trying to fill the tank, and no more raking. When I used the bag on the back, it had to be emptied out every couple of minutes. No more anything. When it comes to fixing the lawnmower, for example, I will admit that I am not the sharpest tool in the shed. Mind you, the push mower has four wheels, not two, and has adjustable heights, unlike the old ones that had only one height. I used it a week or so, and do you know what? It was fun. Although it took me an extra twenty minutes to complete the task, I found it very refreshing. There was no need to rake because the mower gave a finer cut than a gas mower. The noise was next to nothing compared to a gas mower. My last one sounded like in-laws yapping in my ears for about forty-five minutes. The lack of noise means I can cut the grass very early on the weekend without disturbing the neighbours. There are some who do not take that into consideration when doing their own lawns. The great thing about doing the chore so early is I can now throw my golf clubs in the car, go to the range, and hit some balls knowing I already have a bit of work completed under my belt before others even crawl out of bed.

I must let you know about two other benefits I have discovered that are huge for me. One is it is a great workout for the body. That is, after my arms recovered from the first time. Never mind people complaining about the closing of gyms during COVID. Like I have said, just go outside. There are all kinds of alternative ways to keep fit.

The second, and maybe just as important, is the fact that I am doing my part, although small, to help the environment. The fumes and smell from the mower are disgusting, and if we all did a little bit to help the environment, we could make a difference, and it would be a much better place. Climate change is real.

I will probably have the gas mower repaired, and hopefully I will use it only for a back-up in case of any emergency, but for now I am very happy and satisfied that I have invested in a push mower.

Man's Best Friend

Recently, after spending some time with my four-legged friend Chelsea, it has come to me that dogs are the most intellectual, loyal, loving, caring, giving, playful, supportive animals on earth, and they provide unconditional love.

They ask for nothing from us as owners except to be fed, go for a walk, and most importantly be loved, which means to have them beside you when doing nothing else. It can be as much as a car ride (Chelsea rides only shotgun) or a trip to my office (daily routine when Marybel is at work), and even while in my office, she is happy to sit on my chair or stool. The only problem is that when she lies on my stool, I have to work standing up.

Chelsea has also taught me that dogs do know about the time of day. Personally, I get home from the office somewhere between 4:30 and 5:00 p.m. Apparently, she sits on the chair by the front door or on the top of the couch upstairs, looking outside and waiting to see or hear the car come up the driveway. She does the same when Marybel comes home after a twelve-hour shift around 8:30 p.m.

Chelsea knows when it is time to eat both morning and night, and she will let you know by staring at you. If you ignore her, then the barking starts.

The same can be said when she wants some attention. If you ignore her, she will start walking right under your feet and or barking. When you are with her, heaven forbid if you answer the phone. She feels that the phone is taking you away from Chelsea time.

I have been very fortunate that I have never used a leash with her from day one, and she will be twelve years old in the summer of 2022.

Her puppy-dog eyes get to you whenever she gets anxious or nervous, which is applicable when you try to leave the house without her, or when she hears a loud noise or raised voice.

She has the qualities that have inspired me to act accordingly, and I have learned that her traits are what humans should try once in a while—those traits I have mentioned earlier in the book. I am sure others will agree with me about how their dogs are important to them and truly are members of their family. I know mine is.

All of my dogs were special to me, but to be quite honest, even after Chelsea passes—hopefully not for a long time yet—I don't think I will get another four-legged friend like her because I know I have had the best of man's best friend. If you would like a true friend like Chelsea and are thinking of getting a dog for your family, please consider adopting a rescue dog or a mature dog. They deserve a loving home. I can guarantee it will be the best for you and your new best friend.

In the office one day, a co-worker pointed out something that really sums up our four-legged friends. Antonietta gave me permission to use it here in my book: Unconditional love—if you want to give it, have children, and if you want to get it, get a dog. Those are words to live by. Thank you, Antonietta.

Masks

Although I am not a huge fan of wearing a mask, I know it is necessary to protect not only myself but also others around me, younger and older. Everyone must follow the protocol, even if vaccinated—no ifs, ands, or buts. But there is no protocol regarding what you can do to make your mask a little more personal.

There are masks of colour, masks with flowers, masks with pet's faces, masks with stripes, and masks with spots. Heck, I even followed suit and got my own Gordon mask. What I mean is, being part Scottish, I saw a website from a Scottish store in Toronto and in Barrie as well. I got a mask with my name, Gordon, in tartan colours. It was a perfect match to go with my kilt and cap. Now, let's go to the golf courses so I can show off my entire Gordon attire while losing my balls—golf balls, that is. I lost the other ones you were thinking of the day I was married (as most men do).

The only problem with my masks and certain other types, I assume, is that when I put my reading glasses on, they fog up. It is as if I should have wipers on my glasses to clear the fog. I guess the masks are not designed to support glasses. I asked my engineering department to create a pair of wipers on the 3D machine, but all I got was a snicker and probably a thought of "You have got to be kidding me."

Another positive of wearing a mask is you can disguise your real feelings when talking to someone. They don't know whether you are smiling at them, making a face at them, or even sticking your tongue out at them. I have an added bonus, and that is I don't have to wear my dentures on occasions when my mouth is sore from wearing them. Now, I don't have to worry about it when I go to the store, park, or outside where neighbours see me. Just don't get me involved in conversation because it sounds really funny when I talk without my dentures in place.

Money is Not Everything

As humans, we have this tendency to want to have a good life and provide for our family so they don't lack all the extras that were not even in our vocabulary while growing up. That means work hard and make lots of money to not only keep up with the Joneses but also add a whole lot more to their possessions. But that's all they are—possessions. You know, materialistic items that you can't take with you when you're gone.

To get those luxuries, a lot of sacrifice takes place, like working long hours, including weekends and holidays, and for what? To me, most people like to show off these extra materialistic things like bigger homes, fancy cars and boats, eccentric clothes, expensive trips, large and seldom used cottages—the list goes on. Sure, we all would like to have a few more luxuries, myself included, but in all reality, I would not want to sacrifice quality time away from my family just to have bragging rights with my friends, family, or neighbours. Honestly speaking, some of these people must have low self-esteem or are very insecure with what they have. The rest are people who have to be noticed with their materialistic toys or who love to brag. Although I am not the sharpest tool in the shed, I had opportunities to make extra money when I was just starting my family, and I thought that the extra money would come in handy at birthdays and Christmas for my children. I started a part-time, work-from-home estimating service named Terry's Wise Guestimate Service, but not only did it drain me mentally working for three or four contractors at one time, it also pulled me away from the most important possession I had: my family. That included dinners, playing outside with them in the backyard, watching them play organized sports, watching a movie on television with them, or reading a story to them at bedtime. Those are luxuries that I would not give up for anything. If I only knew then what I was sacrificing. The pictures and the memories last a lifetime, and they can be taken with you when your time is up.

I wish some of the people who have the means for all of the extravagance in their lives would stop and put some of their spending to better use, like giving to those less fortunate. It's more rewarding than showing off to others just for bragging rights or your ego.

I am not impressed with money. I am impressed with family. Let us keep in mind the following adages, which we all seem to forget sometimes.

Money is not everything.

Money cannot buy happiness.

Money cannot buy good health.

We all should stop and think about that before it's too late.

Never Grow Up (Totally, That is)

Have you ever witnessed or listened to children play? I mean seriously witnessed or listened. Without being considered a snoop or stalker, I truly enjoy sitting back and watching children play. Let's not forget now that I have helped raise four rug rats of my own, so I have had my share of experience being involved directly and indirectly with children's routines.

They play with creativity, the instinctive ability to appreciate or make good of something (i.e., forts made out of large cardboard boxes or hats, swords made from paper or cardboard, hopscotch on sidewalks, driveways with chalk). Children are great make-believe storytellers, and when they play-act the stories, it is a bonus.

They smile and laugh at times for no other reason other than they feel happy.

All of the above is done without prejudice, without racism, and without hatred. It is plain and simple innocence, and what's wrong with that? Every once in a while, let the inner child inside you come out and play. I know that I do, although sometimes more often than I should, or so I've been told. But I don't care! If it puts you in a happier state of mind, just do it. Nobody else around you will.

Here are a few scenarios that I have personally done to alter my mood from whatever it was to being happy.

1) On a rainy day when my golf game has been cancelled, instead of being upset, I put on a jacket, my ball cap, and an old pair of shoes, and with an umbrella, I go outside and bounce and jump in the puddles, singing an old Gene Kelly tune, "Singing in the Rain."

2) In a crowded environment where I have been stuck in a long line up, instead of getting angry and frustrated, I make funny faces at people looking at me or not. Their reaction to my face makes me laugh.

3) When stressed at work, which happens every once in a while, I have been known to make paper airplanes and direct them towards recycling bins or at the mini basketball net hanging on my office door.

There are dozens more that I have done, but I think you get the picture. As long as no one gets hurt or humiliated, do what you can do to be happy. Children do it all the time, and I think that we adults can learn from a child how to be a child no matter how old we get.

Nice to Read

I cannot speak for everyone regarding what I do in order to alleviate part, if not all, of the stress one can get during the day. Stress could be as simple as a couple of chores to do when you get home to bringing work-related issues home to think about, to some financial implications that are worrisome, to health issues that are bothering you regarding yourself or a loved one.

I have no idea how or when I started to use this idea, but it has been a godsend since I discovered it. I know people close to me are going to say, "You don't even read books, let alone poetry." That's right—poetry.

It took me long enough to realize that I can do or think about only one thing at a time. (I know, it is a male thing.) But after getting into a poem or two, I feel my headache and eye strain begin to ease, and my heart rate slows down a few beats to where I feel relaxed and at peace. On top of that, the poems that I get into also have meaning along with warmth and passion, to the point where I sometimes fall asleep while reading (not out of boredom either).

Some poems are so good that I read them more than once, and all while I am enjoying my evening snack of milk and cookies. I will also be truthful when I say that I have fallen asleep only to wake up later with milk spilt all over my top with cookie crumbs mixed in. Thank goodness that I don't have a cat.

There are so many varieties of poems, but I personally choose to look at inspirational or sometimes humorous ones, and I have even been known to read a few love poems. You would be surprised at how much poetry can make you go into a dream-like mode, which blocks out daily stress. I will also let you in on a little secret, and that is having your partner sit beside you as you read together. Replace the glass of milk with a little red wine, and it could turn out to be a very romantic evening, if you know what I mean.

To my children and grandchildren, I will share some lines of a half dozen of my favourite writings that are very inspirational, including one with a sense of humour. I am sure everyone has a favourite of their own. If not, just try it and allow yourself to pick up a book or read online. I am certain there is a poem that will help you relax and unwind like I have found. I hope you enjoy my favourites.

1) **A poem for personal direction**
   "Always Remember to Forget," by unknown

   Always remember to forget
   The things that made you sad
   But never forget to remember
   The things that made you glad
   Always remember to forget

2) **A poem on finding happiness**
   "Help Yourself to Happiness," by Helen Steiner Rice

   Everybody, everywhere seeks happiness, it's true,
   But finding it and keeping it seem difficult to do.
   Difficult because we think that happiness is found
   Only in places where wealth and fame abound.

   Unaware that happiness is just a state of mind
   Within the reach of everyone who takes time to be kind.
   For in making others happy we will be happy too.
   For the happiness you give away returns to shine on you.

3) **A poem on finding happiness**
    "The Time Is Now," by Betina Van Vaerenbergh

    The time is now
    To find your passion.
    Time waits for no one,
    So get into action.

    To be free of regret.
    In your old age,
    Never, ever forget
    To fully live today!

4) **A famous love poem about the power of small acts of kindness**
    "Just Once," by anonymous

    One step must start each journey.
    One word must start each prayer.
    One hope will raise our spirits,
    One touch can show you care.
    One voice can speak with wisdom,
    One heart can know what's true,
    One life can make a difference,
    You see, it's up to you!

5) **A poem to smile while reading**
    "Laughter Is a Gift," by Catherine Pulsifier

    The most wasted of all days
    Is one where laughter is delayed.
    When life gets you down
    Please don't frown.

    So take this wonderful gift
    And don't' ever be miffed
    Laughter makes living
    For us to be giving.

6) **A few words of wisdom to help defeat stress**
   "A Handful of Laughter," by John McLeod

   Can I give you a handful of laughter
   A smidgen of giggles to boot,

   Can I offer an hourful of happy
   Throw in an odd chuckle or two
   The time spent is worth while
   If the mirth brings a smile
   To the friend I am writing this to

This is a side of me that my family doesn't know, because I have never shared my reading of poems to anyone close. But I find reading poetry to be extremely rewarding and inspirational. I could never write poetry, but I will leave you with a small quote that would suit my style if I could. Although very short in length, it details how I want to be and who I want to be.

   Don't let anyone become a vacuum and suck the happiness
   out of you—pull the plug.

I came across the last quote while looking on the website "Informative Quotes.com". It may be short in length but long in meaning, don't you think?

Nurses

Long before COVID-19 turned our lives upside down—and it will probably have a permanent impact on how we live our lives from this point on—I already knew and very proudly made it clear in my first book how important nurses are. There was a short story using the title "Nurses Are the Best," and it was my personal perspective on what these front-line heroes mean to me.

It is worth repeating and important to emphasize that during this challenging time, nurses have been putting aside their own well-being ahead of anyone during this pandemic of a little over two years. I believe the two-year anniversary was a little over a month ago of my writing this (early February 2022), although it should not be called an anniversary but rather a jail sentence.

Prior to this crippling and devastating pandemic, in my mind nurses are the bread and butter of the healthcare industry. Their professionalism, dedication, compassion, and knowledge come into play every single day of their careers. Personally, I think some nurses know more than some doctors.

On top of their work, they also have to be babysitters to patients who can be demanding at times with miniscule requests just because of their nature. I have no idea how they can put up with the petty and selfish demands that not only patients but also visitors ask for; at times, visitors want more than the patients do. The last time I checked, it is not a hotel. It's a hospital. I probably would have been reprimanded, fired, chastised, or put in a white jacket and charged with assault, because at no time would I put up with the abuse and crazy things that come nurses' way on a daily basis.

Having said that, there is a mental fatigue and stress that is seldom talked about once these heroes leave their place of work. I am quite certain that nurses do not have a shut-off valve when they go home—if they can go home, that is.

Never mind the everyday sights and sounds of hospital trauma that would make any normal human being cringe. Here are some examples of sights and sounds.

1) Victims of car accidents
2) Victims of spousal abuse
3) Victims of rape and sexual abuse
4) Victims of shootings and stabbings
5) Victims of injury during robberies and break-ins
6) Victims of fire
7) Victims of child abuse
8) Victims of injuries in sports
9) Surgery cases and the aftermath
10) Old age (especially now with COVID)
11) Mental issues
12) Birth issues

Many of these examples end up in life-altering conclusions or death.

Now, nurses are to go home to their partner, children, or empty home pretending that everything is OK. They prepare dinners, check their children's homework, and tuck them in bed. In the morning, they make sure their family gets off on the right foot for a great day. I'm sure it even hinders relationships with their significant others. There is not a chance in hell for most of these superheroes to have a normal, happy work-home balance. It's simply not possible.

Nurses have my utmost respect, and if possible, I would like to tell each and every one of them how much they are respected. I wish to thank them in person for all they do. Unfortunately, that is not possible, so I will show it by humbly saying thanks here. I suggest if you have a chance, say thanks to your healthcare workers.

There is one clarification to be made here before I close. Although I mention nurses, all healthcare workers are to be included in the category of respect.

a) Doctors
b) Housekeeping
c) Registration clerks
d) Security
e) Personal support workers
f) Paramedics
g) Social workers

Old Black-and-White Movies

It's only been about two months since I discovered late at night, while I tried but could not fall asleep (which has been happening quite frequently), a network that shows old movies. The youth of today and even their parents may not realize this, but movies used to be in black-and-white. And let me tell you, I honestly appreciate them more today than when I watched them as a kid.

It seems that today's films are based on violence, sex, killing, fast cars, explosions, fighting, drugs, and unbelievable stuff that would not or could not happen in the real world. Unfortunately, it sells. Don't get me wrong; I have tuned into the high-priced, overrated films and enjoyed a few of them. We all need a break from the real world from time to time. But if you stop and think about it, the movies of the past had a believable storyline with actors who actually conversed with each other like normal people. No robots, no talking animals, no ghosts, no witches, no zombies—the list goes on. A big plus is the fact that almost all of the movies had a happy ending, where the good guy triumphed over the bad guy and got the girl.

These films also had morals that we could learn and apply to our way of life as a learning tool. It was also a way to teach our children good values, which seems to be a disappearing scene these days. It amazes me that now, I have a keen eye and notice the actual scene itself. Whether it be inside an office, outside at a sporting event, down the main street of a western town, or in a courtroom, it never ceases to amaze me the reality it brings to the movie. God, I miss some of those movies and TV sitcoms. If you have a chance, do yourself a favour and watch one of these movies. It may surprise you, and you may actually enjoy it.

Earlier tonight, I was fortunate to watch *The Rifleman*, followed by an episode of *Lassie* or *My Three Sons*. Now I will sit down with a cup of tea or a glass of milk, as well as a couple of cookies, and truly enjoy my all-time favourite movie, *The Great Escape*.

On a lighter side, early in the morning, before I leave for the office, I enjoy a few minutes to half an hour watching *The Three Stooges*. It's a great way to start a day with a chuckle, and during these times, we all could use a chuckle or two.

Overdone (TV Shows)

This category that I speak of really irks me. It really drives me crazy.

Why are there so many shows about nothing? Having said that, why does the show Seinfeld come to mind? People who are cast into these roles must be hard up for money or insecure about their own self-being. Just think about it. Who in their right mind would go on the television spilling their guts about their private lives? It is very personal stuff. And the way they dress boggles my mind. At home on a normal day, they are all dolled up. That tends to make me believe that it's made up for TV, with little truth to the show. People who watch these reality shows need to get a life of their own, and they probably have more interesting lives than those they are watching.

I guess by now, it is a well-known fact that I am not a fan of reality shows. In fact, I despise all the crap that these people try to portray.

The following are just a few so-called entertainment shows. There will be no names of shows because it could possibly start a legal issue, and I have no inclination of getting involved in defending myself.

My list of not-so-favourite shows on the boob tube is as follows, is in no particular order.

1) Reality shows
2) Matchmaking shows
3) Vet/animal shows

4)   Cooking or baking shows
5)   Entertainment or talk shows
6)   Dance, singing, and talent shows

With these shows on, they almost make me look forward to the commercials! I never thought I would say that.

Play with Numbers

Here is a simple, off-the-wall list putting something as simple as letters and numbers together, basing them on an event or a series of events. In this case, I chose numbers and songs, movies, and TV sitcoms with a number in them and jotted down good and bad things about each number. Anyone can do this, or maybe I just get bored sitting and had to come up with something to fill my time.

1) "One," by Three Dog Night
   One Flew Over the Cuckoo's Nest (movie, 1975)
   Donald Trump (as in "me first")

2) *Dumb and Dumber* (movie, 1994)
   Donald Trump, Kevin McCarthy

3) *Three Stooges*
   Justin Trudeau, Doug Ford, Donald Trump (again)

4) *4th and Loud* (TV sitcom, 2014)
   Matthew Tkachuk, Brady Tkachuk, Brad Marchand, Brendon Gallagher

5) *The Five Senses* (movie, 1999)
   Touch, sight, hearing, taste, smell

6) *Six Pack* (movie, 1982)
   Bob and Doug McKenzie, brothers
   Fellow Rednecks

7) Seven in Heaven (movie, 2018)
   Mother, George Floyd, Albert Einstein, Charles Darwin, Robin Williams, Martin Luther King Jr., Nelson Mandela

8) *8 Simple Rules* (TV sitcom, 2002–2005)
   Be respectful to others
   Be understanding and compassionate to the less fortunate
   Play for fun and play fair
   Learn with eyes and ears open while mouth is closed
   Be truthful and loving to those close
   Man up to your mistakes
   Don't make promises you can't keep
   Give thanks for what you have

9) *Nine Lives* (movie, 2016), "Nine Lives," Aerosmith, *9 to 5* (movie, 1980)
   Starting positions of the 2017 Houston Astros, who cheated to win the World Series

10) *10 Things I Hate about You* (movie, 1999)
    Racist, sexist, arrogance, egotistic, sarcastic, insecure, hair, weight, a used car salesman, stupid smiles (looks like you're having difficulty going to the washroom). We all know who this is about, don't we?

11) *Ocean's 11* (movie, 2011)
    The Beautiful Game of soccer

12) *The Dirty Dozen* (movie, 1967)
    Kim Jung-Un, N. Korea
    Bashar al Assad, Syria
    Donald Trump, United States
    Alexander Lukashenko, Belarus

White supremacist groups
Anti-environmentalist people
Derek Chauvin, police
Marjorie Taylor Greene, US politician
Ari Nagel, Israel sperm donor
Nathaniel Veltman, Canada
Paul Bernardo, Canadian serial killer
Jeffrey Epstein, financier

Politicians

Have you ever actually watched and listened to politicians? I mean actually watched them up on stage, or at a podium in front of a microphone, and listened to the gibberish spewing out of their mouths.

You give a microphone to any politician, and he thinks he has the answer to everything wrong and will promise you the world if you elect him into office. Unfortunately, once in the position of power, along with his big office and perks at the taxpayers' expense, somehow, he forgets the people who put him on the illustrious pedestal. On top of that, all of his promises are forgotten as well.

It's oh so much fun to watch them talk about what they can do, and often some of their so-called solutions have merit. The only problem is that it will take time and a lot of money, if it ever happens at all. My only issue is "Who is going to pay for it?" and without hesitation, the answer is quite simple: you and me, the taxpayers.

Also, think for a moment about what they are trying to say and what they propose to do for you if elected. This applies especially to incumbents, the ones who have been in power for quite some time. My observation and question to them is, "What the hell have you been doing since in office? The promises and proposals are similar to what you mentioned when you first got elected." It's as if they went to their filing cabinet, pulled out the file that said "Speech," blew off the dust, changed the date, and said the same crap all over again. Do they think they can pull the wool over our eyes? We are not as stupid and gullible as they think we are.

The only thing funnier is watching two or more politicians in a debate. Everyone talks while nobody listens. They point fingers at each other, raise their voices to the point of yelling, show disrespect to each other by throwing insults, and make sarcastic comments towards each other. Temper tantrums are quite common in these debates. I swear that politicians put more effort and time into this rhetoric rather than telling you what the problems are and how they will try to fix them if elected.

Watching politicians talk is like watching five-year-olds argue. Children say things at times but for the most part resolve their issues rather quickly and move on playing together in harmony.

The only difference between politicians and children is that children are young, innocent, and immature. The word *immature* applies to children (who do not know any better), not politicians (who should know better).

Prima Donnas

The definition of *prima donna* is "a vain or undisciplined person who finds it difficult to work under direction or as part of a team." The word *selfish* also comes to mind.

At least two sports come to mind when the phrase *prima donna* is used. One is tennis.

Have you ever watched any of these games without wanting to take some of the players aside, give them a slap, and tell them to grow up? Whenever they lose a game, a set, or a match, they blame everyone around them except themselves. They have yelled—no, screamed—at the linesman, umpire, and officials over what they think is a bad or missed call. They have smashed tennis balls in every direction over a bad or missed call, or a missed shot by themselves, which is commonly known as an unforced error. They have destroyed their racquets by smashing them on the court repeatedly until it is no longer a tennis racquet. And they'll destroy more than one racquet at the same time. I have seen some players throw what is in their bag that they bring with them on the court before the match. Things like water bottles, towels, attire, and more fly all over, including the chair. Heck, there are even a couple of players who shall be left anonymous who have whacked their heads a few times with their racquet to the point of cutting their foreheads open, with blood dripping down their face. And what's with the noise issue? There seems to be a double standard with it comes to noise. These prima donnas require the crowd to be quiet while the match is going on, and if someone sneezes or coughs, just listen to the words that are thrown at them, or even worse, the evil stare. In contrast, the sounds the players make when they return a shot can be summed up as follows: They sound like they are either having an orgasm, or they are on the toilet grunting because they are having trouble going number two. I honestly think those players are full of shit!

The other sport that comes to mind is golf. This group of prima donnas also has to have quiet while playing the game. I've seen players get unruly with words or that evil stare. They even have officials holding up signs to keep people quiet while they hit the ball. And heaven forbid if you make any kind of movement. What I cannot understand is why they take so long to hit the ball. And what is with all the practice swings before they hit the ball? Heck, they don't even carry their own golf bags; someone else is delegated to walk around carrying the clubs. Are they afraid to carry their own bags, or do they worry about what it looks like to others, almost like this is demeaning to their ego? And what's with the look after they miss a short putt? Some look again as if they have a second chance to make the same putt. I cannot for the life of me figure out that one. Even if they play that same hole the following day, the hole is then moved to another part of the green, and what are the chances of hitting the ball to the exact same spot for a similar putt, even if the flagstick remained in the same spot? It boggles my mind.

There are other sports where things are not kosher, such as hockey, where good players are not called for penalties, and even if denied, it is rather obvious that it is a cardinal rule not to touch those prima donnas because if you do, you are in the box for two minutes. Those players whine as well as tennis players when things don't go their way.

There are other sports as well, but to me, tennis and golf are the sports best-known for prima donnas!

QAnon

To be quite frank—and please excuse my lack of knowledge—how in the heck did the word *QAnon* become such a conspicuous topic?

It's unprecedented. I have heard that word so much, I finally have a chance to use it.

I honestly did not know that the word QAnon existed, never mind knowing what it means. After hearing all of what it represents and some of the conspiracy theories involved, I have come to a conclusion that the people who actually believe in these theories are either brain-dead, are in need of help by means of therapy, or are already beyond help. Maybe these people stood out of the room when they were handing out brains, or the warranty expired on their brains, and they forgot to have it replaced.

I mean, have you heard some of these theories?

- COVID-19 was created in a lab in China.
- A group of Satan-worshipping elites who run a child sex ring are trying to control our politics and media.
- Humans do not play a significant role in climate change.
- Several mass shootings in recent years were staged hoaxes.

These concepts and many others are baseless theories, and one would have to be a total idiot to think there is any truth to these theories. I thought my American neighbours were smarter than that. But like the former president said during his election run (and yes, he is the former president), "I like the uneducated people." I guess a good percentage of these people believe in the QAnon theory. It's too bad because I love the United States, a great place to visit, and the people are very proud, friendly, and accommodating. But to those few who believe in the QAnon garbage, get a life—and while you're at it, go to Walmart and see if you can get a good deal on a brain. Even a used one would be better than the one you have now.

QTL

Sit for a moment and ponder over the above three letters. Try to figure out what they stand for. To tell the truth, I never would have thought to put the letters together, never mind what they mean.

That is until one night, when I was bored, picked up the TV remote and started flipping through the channels trying to find something to watch (without commercials, that is) to put me to sleep. I came across some sort of sports award show already in progress.

Jimmy Johnson (from the Dallas Cowboys) was being inducted into the Football Hall of Fame and was giving his acceptance speech. All of a sudden, he stood still, looked directly towards the audience, and uttered the three letters very clearly and carefully: "QTL." Then he expanded the letters into three words: "Quality time left." He wasn't talking about anything to do with sports but more about how much quality time that we have left to enjoy what is and should be close to all of us. That is family. It made me stop and think for a moment.

The average age for a Canadian man is 79.9 years, and it is 84 years for a Canadian woman. Using simple math and my own age of 69, it means that I have just over 10 years to enjoy my family, friends, and Mother Earth and all that its beauty has to offer. Maybe it's about time to think about retirement and concentrate on what I preach, and that is to enjoy my family a whole lot more, spend quality time with them to share some laughs and hugs, spend time with friends to reminisce about the past and catch up with what's happening today, and do a lot more of the "me" things that have been put aside. In my case, that means putting my cameras in a bag and then in a car, plane, train, boat, or bike, heading somewhere to indulge myself with beautiful landscape, wildlife, and people. Then I will bring the photos and memories back home to share.

There is so much beauty in the world, and I want to see, hear, and learn as much as I can while I can. Let's not forget that things change in a hurry as we get older.

Jimmy Johnson, I would like to thank you for this wake-up call with those three letters, QTL. Those three letters may be short in length, but they are long in stature. It's made me stop and think about the present and what I want the future to bring. Like others, I have worked relatively hard for over fifty-five years to provide for my family and get to a place that is comfortable. The time is now (albeit behind schedule) to seriously put my next, and probably my last, phase of life into action. Like I have said on many occasions, life is short and can be ended in a moment's notice. Maybe you should stop and think about this as well.

Quatrain

A quatrain is a verse with four lines.

Before any more is said about the word *quatrain*, I shall confess that I was looking forward to having a little fun with rhymes, and I discovered that quatrain means a verse with four lines. It's not that I knew what it meant but more that I was looking for a synonym for poems, and guess what? There are different terms for poetry based on the number of words, syllables, and lines. Who knew?

Here are just a few examples of poems.

> Haiku: 17 syllables arranged in three lines of 5, 7, and 5 syllables

> Cinquain: poetic forms that employ a 5-line pattern that describes a person, place, or thing

> Stanza: a group of lines in a poem

I could go on, but I am getting away from the real reason why poetry is here. It is a stress relief, and you would be surprised what you can come up with. It's a unique way of expressing yourself, or in my case, a way of expressing funny facts. It is a viable alternative to what is happening right now.

During the COVID crisis, I will take anything to help alleviate the worries and anxiety of not being able to do much, not being able to see friends and family, and the mental fear of being alone. If only for a moment, it can take away a little sadness and depression that we are all feeling during this time. You might even discover a hidden talent you never knew about. Think about the fun you can have with it.

A few of my short rhymes are as follows.

Jingle bells, jingle bells,
Jingle all the way,
Oh what fun it is to ride
In grandma's Chevrolet

There once was an old man that I knew.
I noticed him while at Walmart.
Although he seemed proud and humble,
Man, oh man, could he let go a fart!

Jesus walks the water.
He's the lifeguard at our pool.
Donald J. Trump
Is the world's biggest fool.

Hi-ho, hi-ho,
It's off to work I go.
They ring the bell,
I work like hell,
Hi-ho, hi-ho, hi-ho, hi-ho.

My Bonnie lies over the ocean.
My Bonnie lies over the sea.
My Bonnie lies over the ocean,
So please give her beer over to me.

These are meaningless little rhymes, but they could help pass the time while being alone. If you want to change it up a bit, try to make a warm and sincere poem. I haven't gone that far yet, but let's give it a try.

> *There once was a lady from Nantucket*
> *Who …*

No, let's not go any further. I think there could be a not-so-proper ending, and this is a family book.

Quiche

Although it was a very long time ago—approximately forty years, give or take a few—an innocent prank played on a future brother-in-law comes to mind periodically and still brings a little chuckle.

While at a family function, of which there were many, we were standing in line at a buffet set up in one of the in-law's houses. The future brother-in-law (name to be left anonymous) reached out and picked up a plate with something on it that I had never seen before. As he brought the plate back towards his tray, somebody mentioned, "Real men don't eat quiche." The plate went right back on the counter where it came from in record speed. He carried on as if nothing had happened, but if I am not mistaken, he made it clear to all around by showing his beer bottles while walking back to his seat. To be quite honest, I still would not recognize quiche even if it bit me in the butt. I do know that it is classified as a French tart filled with cheese, vegetables, and sometimes meat. Although I did not say, "Real men don't eat quiche," I refuse to go near the stuff and will sternly refuse if offered to me.

The same can be said about light beer. Our group of four golfers always enjoy a drink along with a few minutes of laughs after every round, and it is now an ongoing thing that when Kiran orders a light beer, Nam and I make a comment: "Light beer is for girls." It's an inside joke between the four of us. I should not talk because although I may say the comment, I have a non-alcoholic drink to be social, but also because my drive home is not a short one, and I take the statement "If you drink, don't drive" very seriously.

To me, the same could be said about specialty coffee shops. There are too many to name, but it should be pretty obvious as to which ones I am talking about. If I want to have a coffee, I want to have a coffee that actually smells, looks like, and tastes like—you guessed it—coffee, not some fruity scent that has every colour of the rainbow in it with what looks like shaving cream on top. Not for me, thanks. While we are at it, don't get me started with plant-based burgers. No matter what anyone says, there is a difference in the look and definitely the taste. No disrespect to the vegans who go for it, but I want real meat in my burger, and for your information, the creature that is in my burger or on my plate, while alive, grazed on and ate grass at one time, so I can say that my meat is also plant-based. Put that in your veggie burger!

Racism

Why does the topic of racism, which is part of a bigger and not so nice category known as prejudice still exist in our society today? It seems like every day, we hear about an act of racism—and not only towards colour, race, and gender. Now it seems there are groups that have hatred towards anything that they don't agree with. Just look at the insurrection that took place in the United States on January 6, 2021, as an example. Why?

I do have my issues with certain policies and lawmakers. But even though I disagree, they are in place for a reason, and therefore I must abide by these rules and laws. If not, there should be a discussion to clear up the law or make additional or alternate proposals in order to benefit everyone. If that does not work, then the next step is to get a lobbyist or a group of people and organize a peaceful rally in order to be heard. Then and only then can the discussions take place. No looting, no weapons, and no destruction of private property, because we all lose when that happens.

These rallies are important because voices need to be heard. There is too much hatred towards humankind. Personally, I love and respect everyone unless you hurt my family physically, emotionally, or financially, and then I can and will be your worst nightmare—legally, that is.

There is so much hatred with it comes to the following.

1. Religion
2. Gender
3. Colour

4. Nationality
5. Sexuality
6. Bullying
7. Mental issues
8. Spousal abuse
9. Child abuse
10. Heredity

There should be no leniency for people who commit crimes of hatred and racism. If you are white, black, pink with purple polka dots, women, man, transgender, thin, not so thin, young, or old; if you have same-sex partners, drive a lemon, drive a BMW, go to church to pray, do not go to church, the consequences for your crimes against anyone just mentioned should be the same. No ifs, ands, or buts. We all should be able to lead happy and safe lives no matter who we are.

Even if you can afford the best lawyer around, or have no lawyer, the consequences for your crime should be the same—no deals to be made, no early release for good behaviour, no retrials (appeals), no pardons to be made. You do the crime, you do the time.

You should be judged by the public and your peers, not in front of a hand-picked jury or with a fancy man with an ego who uses big words that mean nothing but sarcasm (aka lawyer).

That's just me letting off steam. There are so many injustices in this world, and it is only getting worse. Let's fix the problem now. We cannot undo the past, but we can try to make amendments now so it is fair for all—and I mean all.

Residential Schools

After hearing about this recently and following it in the news for a while (it is normally against my principles to watch the news because for the most part, the news is bias and one-sided, and it is depressing to hear about how our world is going down the crapper), I have come to the conclusion that the Indigenous people have been vastly mistreated again, to say it mildly. This time, it's the children. Before I go any further, I will say that I am proud to be Canadian and will be the first to wave the flag on special occasions. I will always stand and sing the national anthem when I hear it being played.

Unfortunately, after hearing the history regarding the children who went to these residential schools, it is very disheartening and troublesome that this could happen, and it did happen. It makes me a little sad and at the same time quite angry that it happened right here in Canada—and not only in one spot but right across this country. To add salt to the wound, it was covered up by those who were to protect, teach, and nurture these innocent children, not physically and sexually abuse these gifts from God.

The children were taken away from their parents at a very vulnerable, young age only to be put into these residential schools. Then they were abused, starved, beaten, and ultimately killed and buried in mass gravesites, to be forgotten. Why? Because they were Indigenous people, not worthy of a free and accepting life we all have and take for granted. This actually compares this to the Holocaust: innocent people who were killed for no reason whatsoever.

Shame on those responsible for being part of this tragedy that occurred while under the watchful eye of those who we trusted to do the right thing. Whether it be the church, the elected officials, or anyone else involved, someone should show some dignity and accept responsibility. At least show compassion and apologize to not only the Indigenous people here in Canada but also the rest of the world, saying that what we did was wrong, and we are sorry for what happened. That would be a necessary start for healing.

Although I heard the government will look into it, we all know what that means. They will drag their feet (that's the nice word I will use; there is another one) with words to keep us informed that they care, but talk is cheap. I truly believe that everyone involved is hoping that it will be forgotten over time and be swept under the rug, just like every other matter pertaining to the Indigenous—you know, stolen land, invasion of their land, lack of clean drinking water, racial comments, lack of medical care, and let's not forget the disappearance and killing of Indigenous women. I could be here all day talking about the way they have been mistreated, but unfortunately it will probably fall on deaf ears. After all, I am only one person. I truly hope others will take a stand, and maybe, just maybe, change will occur.

I will sum up what I feel and believe: "I am truly sorry for what you have gone through, for what you are going through. My thoughts and prayers go out to you, and I wish everyone can be treated equally with respect, kindness, love, opportunity, and compassion." After all, around the world, Canadians are known for these qualities and then some. So, let's start showing the qualities to our fellow Canadians, especially to the original Canadians, and our Indigenous family.

Retirement

Where in the heck did this word come from? I mean, it seemed like yesterday that I picked up a mechanical pencil and started my career as a draftsman at a scaffolding company down by the CNE in Toronto, and now this word *retirement* is becoming more prominent in discussions.

I honestly never even thought of this word until my best friend of over fifty years started his retirement a few years back. That made me think, "Hey, I am not that far behind him."

Yasu enjoys himself because he has worked so hard for so many years and deserves to be spoiled with happy times, but I am not sure that I want to retire any time soon. Let me clarify: maybe not work full time—you know, eight hours a day five days a week minimum for fifty-two weeks a year. It would be nice to help others, like volunteer at a hostel or an animal rescue for one day a week, but hopefully I will try to work part time for two to three days a week. That would serve a dual purpose. First, it would allow me to enhance my days of leisure to not only enjoy life (financially) a little more, but just as important, if not more so, it would act as a stimulant to my little brain, and we all can use that. I know I could. Personally, I have seen people who retire cold turkey and do nothing after they hang up their work responsibilities, and they go downhill very quickly; their life is now meaningless, and they go through the motions for the remainder of their days. I guess that because I have worked one way or another since I turned fourteen, retirement is not part of my vocabulary, although early planning has been on my mind for a while now.

A hobby is important, so continuing to play with my grandchildren and indulge in my 3D wood puzzles, plus increasing my favourite hobby of photography outdoors, will play a prominent role. A day or two of volunteering should help pass the time. I can't forget about playing golf with my favourite golfers, Yasu, Kiran, and Nam. They have a positive outlook on life, and they always leave the course after a round with a smile and contentment knowing it was a day well spent. I can't say the same about how I play the game, but that's another story. Adding a few days of part-time work would add to my longevity and is guaranteed to leave with a smile on my face and fulfilment in my heart.

Scottish Godfather

I have been in construction for all of my fifty plus years in the workforce, and over that length of time, I have come across diverse groups of people. In this case, I mean nationalities.

As we all know, our country, like a lot of others, was built by immigrants, and in this case, I am speaking of Italians. They are the hardest working, family-oriented people who sacrificed everything to make a better life for themselves and their families. Most came here with nothing more than the shirts on their backs. Without those people, Canada would not be what it is today, and for that I am forever grateful.

However, you learn about other groups that do things for a better life, but maybe, just maybe, in a different fashion. With the Italians, there is this stigma related to the Mafia. That's where I heard another meaning for the word *godfather*.

This family and related groups were included in criminal activities for the longest time, but I did a little research and discovered that there is a Scottish godfather named Arthur Thompson of Springburn, Glasgow, Scotland. He was born September 1931, and died March 13, 1993, at the age of sixty-one.

The following is a brief summary of his activities.

- Started as a money lender, and to those who did not repay their debts, he would literally nail them to floors and doors.
- Protection rackets soon followed, along with robberies and heists.
- Invested his money into legitimate business, which grew over the years. His earnings were about one hundred thousand pounds a week as a loan shark.
- Had a bomb explode under his car and narrowly escaped, but his mother-in-law was killed.
- Later, he spotted two men whom he suspected of the bombing, and he forced their van off the road and into a lamp post, killing both.
- He was charged with murder, but nobody would testify against him.
- Even his wife, Rita, went to the home of one of the two and stabbed the wife. She served three years.
- Grandchildren and great-grandchildren have to remain anonymous for their own safety.
- Two other attempts were made on his life. He was shot in the groin outside his home, the Ponderosa in Provanmill, named after a ranch from a western TV series, *Bonanza*. He was also run over by a car intentionally which broke his leg and shot once again.
- His son, Arthur Jr. (nicknamed Fat Boy) died after being shot three times. A former enforcer named Paul Ferris was arrested.
- Two of Ferris's associates were killed and placed on the road of Arthur Jr.'s funeral procession.
- There was also a bomb scare at the cemetery.
- Arthur Thompson died of a heart attack on March 13, 1993, after thirty years of being involved in the criminal world.
- Rumoured to have been involved in the 1963 Great Train robbery when 2.6 million pounds (about 30 million pounds today) was stolen from the Glasgow to London mail train.

I honestly thought I would have loved to be around during those times. Now, knowing that Scotland has had their share of similar activities, I am kind of envious. I know that I am a proud Canadian being born in the heart of Canada's largest city, Toronto, but my father came from a small port area in the north of the city of Edinburgh, Scotland, known as Leith, so I do have a little bit of Scottish blood and am also proud to have that as well.

But now that I know about the Scottish godfather, I think I have a new folk hero.

Sneeze, Cough, and Fart

The old adage goes that man cannot do two things at a time (properly, anyway), and I have to agree.

As an example, I will use myself so as not to expose anyone else. It's also a well-known fact that men will never admit to miscues, especially this kind.

Numerous times while walking down the hallway with my favourite cup of coffee, I notice that behind me is a trail of drops of coffee on the floor. To help resolve that issue, my cup is never filled to the brim anymore, always a few mouthfuls short to alleviate the spills. There is also talking on the cell phone while pumping gas. I know it's a no-no, but I am sure I am not the only one. After filling up the car, getting the receipt, and heading out of the station, it was pointed out to me by a horn from another motorist that I had not put my cap back on the tank. It is kind of embarrassing, to say the least. On top of that, there was a time when I left my gloves on top of the garbage bin, but at least I remembered on my own to go back within a few minutes to retrieve them before they disappeared forever.

And let's not get involved with talking about reading and walking up or down a flight of stairs at the same time.

Now for the title of this story, "Sneeze, Cough, and Fart." Although it is a gift, or more probably one of my many useless talents, I can proudly say that I can do three things at a time. Sometimes I can do it without warning of it coming and without any practice. The only problem is that I don't know where to put the Kleenex first. It's kind of like doing the game *Rock, Paper, Scissors*. You know, you don't know which direction to stick your fingers (with or without Kleenex) in order to win the moment. Having said that, I think I have to go visit the washroom now because nature is calling.

Sunrises and Sunsets

The most beautiful way to begin a day is with a sunrise, and the best way to end a day is with a sunset. I am in awe every time I am blessed to witness the spectacle of the beauty and serenity of a sunrise, and will not hesitate to watch it. Even when I have been driving early in the morning, there have been times that I have pulled over to the shoulder and watched for a few minutes; if the camera is in the car, that is a bonus. Believe it or not, every sunrise is different. Seeing them brings a sense of beauty and mystery of life, and it always adds a bit of energy to me to start my day on a bright note (no pun intended). The same can be said about sunsets, which provides a feeling of peacefulness, tranquillity, and warmth, and in many cases a chance of romance if the setting permits. I remember those days a long, long time ago. Never miss a chance to watch a sunrise or a sunset. I know I don't.

Like everyone else who travels, memories are brought back with pictures to share with family and friends and to reminisce years later.

In my prized photos, there will always be pictures of sunrises and sunsets of every place I have visited. Every one is different. Whether they can be seen as close as my home or as far away as ballooning over the Serengeti in Tanzania, Africa, each and every one of them is picturesque.

Taxes

I am absolutely certain that I am not alone regarding the word *taxes* and the headaches and heartaches it gives whenever the word is used, which is every day of our lives if you think about it.

We all work our backsides off to provide for our family. First, we get taxed on our hard work, which can be quite substantial. Then what is left to bring home is now to be used for the three basics for your family, which are food, clothing, and a roof over their head.

Now there's tax on food, tax on travel (hotel and airfare), tax on clothes, property tax on our home, tax on home utilities, tax on insurance (to protect your home), and tax on gas (to help you get to work or stores). If I am correct, there is tax on top of tax, and tax on activities (kids, adults—it doesn't matter). Tax, tax, tax! It's a vicious cycle, and most of the tax goes to the government. What do they do with it all? Every time there seems to be a deficit or their books are showing how much they owe, all they simply have to do is raise our taxes in order to pay to get the debt down or paid off. I have an idea. How about if we consumers find ourselves overwhelmed or getting deeper into debt due to mortgage, car payments, food, and the like, why don't we withhold or pay fewer taxes to get ourselves out of debt? It is such a simple solution to a never-ending problem that many people are finding themselves in today, especially since the COVID crisis. I don't think the powers that be would even consider it. But as the old adage goes, "What's good for the goose is good for the gander."

I even put forth a suggestion to the owner a while ago for a new workweek proposal. Instead of working five days with two days off (weekend), why not have a two-day workweek with five days off (long weekend), but I guess that I pushed it too far as I also added that our pay remains the same. It didn't quite get the response I was hoping for, but no harm in trying.

Teachers

Every industry has its ups and downs, but since this COVID pandemic started over two years ago, the ups and downs that seemed like molehills have become mountains. Just look at the small businesses that had to close—and for a lot, that could not reopen. The education sector was also turned upside down.

I personally have a soft spot for the education sector and have the utmost respect and compassion for what teachers are going through. I know that I have joked with teachers over the past about two months off in the summer and that they have Christmas and Easter breaks along with a shortened day of work in the classroom. But that's only in fun with a few friends who are in that line of work.

My wake-up call to how hard they work to teach our children was when I became part of the parent-teacher committee of my daughter's school about twenty-five years ago, give or take a couple of years. That was when I found out how challenging and demanding their job was. The preparation time before and after class, the research that has to be done for the subject they teach, report cards, being a nurse and disciplinarian, parent-teacher interviews, extracurricular activities, yard duty—the list is never ending.

Now, on top of that, they have to have the patience, the energy, and the compassion to teach the children so they understand what they are being taught. Teachers have to put up with sick kids, students who may talk back, students who don't know when to keep quiet or when to put their cell phones away, and students with every excuse feasible as to why the homework assignment is not complete. Once again, the list is endless. Plus, let's not forget the parents. They can also be a thorn with their petty complaints. I honestly do not know how they do it, and for the most part, they do it with dignity and grace because they also show the children that teachers lead by example.

If I were a teacher, I would probably be a permanent resident in a mental institute, living in a room with padded walls and in a straitjacket. Oh, I almost forgot: with the addition of COVID, now they have to teach online to students. I wish the government would do the following simple changes to benefit the teachers, who in my book are greatly underpaid and underappreciated.

1) Reduce class sizes
2) Increase their salary
3) Make up your mind on schools closing or opening

These are simple solutions to benefit the teacher. All kidding aside, I personally love teachers and all they do for our children. They have my utmost respect, compassion, and admiration for the job they do. My four children prove that teachers do their job well, and for that I am eternally grateful.

Thank you to each and every teacher out there.

Ten Rules

There are a lot of theories, instruction, and opinion about how to have a meaningful, rewarding, and happy life. Although similar, I have my own version that enriches my life, and hopefully I have made a difference in others' lives and put smiles on their faces, even if just for a moment.

I would like to share the following.

1. **Treat others with respect and dignity**
   This should be a no-brainer. If you want to be treated with respect, you must first show the same towards others. We all deserve to be treated this way.

2. **Have compassion and understanding towards those less fortunate**
   It's not acceptable to make fun of, insult, or ignore those less fortunate than us. They have been dealt a bad hand for whatever reason or have other issues they won't talk about. They have their reasons, and who am I to judge? That's why I make time to chat or just give a friendly smile in greeting as I pass by. If you have a problem doing that, then maybe you have an issue.

3. **Give thanks and praise**
   Why do we complain about the things (mostly materialistic, anyway) that we do not have? Why must we complain about others who seem to be doing better? I am thankful for what I have and what I have done, with absolutely no jealousy or animosity towards anyone. Maye we all should be a little more thankful.

4. **Donate or volunteer to a cause**

   Giving money to a good cause always provides a good feeling, but you would be surprised how that feeling is magnified when you volunteer in person. It is much more rewarding, and there is a variety of places to do so. From pet shelters to hostels, to hospitals, to helping street people, to helping in senior residences, to woman's shelters and youth centres, to getting involved in fundraising for a good cause like the Salvation Army or church events, they are always appreciated. So many places require the help of volunteers. I have dabbled in all that I have mentioned, with the exception of an animal shelter, which I probably will do when I retire. Volunteering is a commitment, so I have learned to be responsible. People depend on you, but it sure is worth it to me.

5. **Play for fun, and play fair**

   This is simple. So many people, young and old, seem to have to win no matter what the game is or whom they are playing against. Some even resort to cheating. My simple philosophy is if you are not getting paid to play, then play for fun. My children were taught that from a very early age, and it shows today. It works for not only playing games but also with other aspects to create a healthier and happier life.

6. **Learn by keeping your eyes and ears open and your mouth shut**

   How many times has someone been so busy talking about anything that they miss the importance of where they are and what they are looking at? How many times have you heard someone ask for an explanation or an answer to a question asked after the same question has already been answered, especially in a tour group?

7. **Think before you speak**

   Everyone is guilty of this. You speak but without thinking first, which in some cases is an admission of guilt. Just like when children say, "I didn't do it," it really means, "I did it, but to you I didn't do it."

8. **Be proud of who you are and what you have accomplished, but do it with humility**

We all want to climb the ladder of success. It comes with prestige, status, financial gains, and security, and we can buy neat stuff with the money we have. If we are blessed with a God-given talent, then we can show it off for a financial gain. But it is not right to brag about all you have done and what you have. I have more respect for the person who has humility and does not brag or show off all he has. To me, bragging is a sign of insecurity. Humility is a strength, and you can tell who has it and who doesn't.

9. **Walk the walk, not just talk the talk**

Too many people talk too much about what they are going to do, what they are going to see, whom they are going to help, and how much of a donation they are going to give—and then they do not fulfill the promise. As the sayings go, talk is cheap, actions speak louder than words. Another saying is short and to the point: Just do it. If you do not have the intention of following through, then just shut up!

10. **If you have nothing nice to say, say nothing at all**

What is the purpose of degrading, insulting, or being sarcastic towards others when they have done nothing to you personally? Besides, there are always two sides to a story, and who says your story is correct. If others are not there to be allowed a response, I find that repulsive. Don't forget that someone can say the same thing about you, and we all know that we would not want to hear it. "I can go to bed every night knowing that I have not hurt anyone physically, financially, or mentally" are words to live by.

UFC

I really don't understand this so-called sport of ultimate fighting. To me, it's just a couple of people with a few more muscles and a few less brain cells than most of us trying to beat each other to a pulp to wear a belt similar to the wrestling organizations.

We all know that wrestling is a little entertaining, with all the drama of a TV show; maybe it is closer to a reality sitcom. As we also know the stories are fabricated to grab viewers' interests.

The so-called sport of UFC is not entertaining. It's simply one ugly person trying to beat another ugly person into submission, or they spoon each other on the canvas, or they try to smash their opponent's face so when it's over, the loser is now uglier than the winner. Have you seen some of these fighters? Talk about ugly. In a beauty contest, even Rodney Dangerfield would take first place. Sum up the value to the viewer. It costs a pretty penny to watch it live and the main event in some matches lasts less than a minute. That's less than an annoying commercial. And don't forget to look at the place they do this barbaric act of Neanderthal fighting. There are enough blood trails and blood in the ring to do a transfusion on someone in need.

I will say that they are quite fit, and I am impressed with the training and hard work that is put into these athletes, but for goodness' sake, put it to better use. Why go through all the training, but at the end of your career, all you have to show for it is a belt and maybe—no, probably—a broken nose that cannot be straightened out, incoherent responses to simple questions like "How much is two plus two?" and trouble speaking like an adult?

Of course, there are exceptions to this rule, but they are few and far between, and that's for the winners. What about the majority of the fighters who are quickly forgotten? I have my own definition for UFC: Useless Fighting Clowns.

Update Eulogy

This is a simple chore for me because it is already in the works. What I mean to say is my eulogy is being done by me! This way, there will be no work for anyone at the funeral service.

A lot of thought was put into it, but it is actually quite easy to do. All that is needed is a chair, a tripod, and a video camera with a good memory card to record. Oh, I almost forgot the most important material to work with: paper and a pen to write things down as they happen so events will be easier to speak about when recording. It may be a month or so between my recording sessions, but it's getting done. Hopefully I can continue to do this with the keen interest I do now.

I think it would be a good deed to share my positive thoughts in a video for anyone who may not be having a good day. But the reality is it is being done for my children and grandchildren, and I hope I can be a little inspiration for them after I have left and put a smile on their faces. For that reason alone, I will keep doing what I am doing. Oh, as far as the revision goes, there will be no negative words said about anyone.

Like I mentioned in my first book, I can go to sleep knowing I have not hurt anyone physically, emotionally, or financially, and I am at peace with that. I also know that if I do anger or upset anyone, that is tough for them because I won't be able to hear them—I will already be in a permanent sleep.

Vastly Overrated

To me, this topic could be applicable to a whole bunch of people or groups of people. I will give you my reasons why I believe they are overrated, based on personal observations.

1) **Athletes:** Overpaid prima donnas, to say the least. They continuously ask for more money even after they have had a bad season. Why can't owners decrease the salary based on a bad performance? But it does not work that way. The majority of players are overrated and overpaid with egos that are out of control. Unfortunately, the fans are the ones who pay for it, and they pay dearly to watch.

2) **Hospital CEOs:** Again, these people think they are above everyone else, especially in the income category. If correct in what I have heard, a CEO makes more money in one morning by lunch than the average hard worker makes in a year. Let's not even talk about the bonuses—not worth it.

3) **Actors and actresses:** For the majority of these people, they are overpaid and overrated with egos so big, it's a wonder their heads don't explode. Just look at them on talk shows and award shows. They are dressed to kill, trying to outdo others dressed at these shows. The majority of what they talk about is themselves. "Me, me, me," comes to mind. You can tell how full of you-know-what an actor is when he or she says, "I took the role after reading the script because I felt the part," or, "I believe a voice has to be heard," when in reality they accept the part because they need the pay cheque. That was said by another actor, not me.

4) **Lawyers:** I could be here all day talking about lawyers, but the more I say, the more that can be used against me in a lawsuit. So, all I will say is that lawyers are overpaid based on what I have heard. And I love it when a lawyer says, "We don't get paid until you get paid." That may be true, but check out the percentage they take when they win a case for you. Normally it is as much as, if not more than, what you take. As the saying goes, 40 per cent for you and 60 per cent for me. Guess which one of those two amounts is yours, and which one is the lawyer's take? I think you got this one without any help.

5) **Titles after a name:** Why do people have to put initials or titles after their name? Whether it be an email, a letter, or anything that leaves their desk, they won't let the piece of paper leave their desk without some sort of added letters, as if it was on their birth certificate or passport. To me, it's a sign of total insecurity, and it is meaningless at times. I wonder whether these people also use the names or initials on birthday cards they send to their children.

Vegetarian (Not)

After you read and make a decision about my perspective on vegetarians or those pretending to be vegetarians, let's not jump the gun just yet. Those who say they eat only organic are in this category as well, although there may be some truth with health benefits to a lifestyle that does not include meat as a staple. I find it hard to believe the health benefits outweigh the satisfaction of a great-tasting piece of meat such as a steak, hamburger, or meat lover's pizza. Especially when the steak is served with a helping of potatoes covered in gravy. Add a little salt, and let's not forget the buttered bun to mop up the remaining gravy. Or a nice, cold beer with a pizza being shared with friends. Plant-based bacon is not even a consideration. I guess what I am trying to say is life is short enough as it is, and I plan to enjoy it to the fullest. Whether it be with travel, family, friends, or in this case food, I will choose my own diet, and when I go, I am going to go with a full belly and a smile on my face.

Plus, I don't want to hear about living longer with a meatless lifestyle. As long as you eat responsibly and exercise, which is as simple as going for a walk, there is a good chance you will live a long, healthy, and happy life. Hell, my father smoked a pack of cigarettes a day, drank like a fish at times, and ate only meat for his meals, and he passed away at the age of ninety-three.

The main reason for my dislike of vegetarian food is the veggie alternative to meat. It is a plant-based mix that is supposed to replicate meat. Well, let me tell you that it doesn't even come close to meat. It tastes more like fertilizer, or a bad attempt of certain foods that you just chew and chew but are afraid to swallow.

I had that experience when I accidently bought the wrong package of hamburger meat patties, and because I don't like to throw away food, I decided to try them. After about five minutes of this abomination of stuff in my mouth, I knew this was not for me. It took a full five minutes to get the nerve to swallow and another thirty minutes to finish the patty. It was so bad that I would eat my own cooking instead of that poor alternative to meat. Yeah, it was that bad. There is no way they can invent an alternative to real meat.

Making matters worse are the people who pretend and publicly say they are vegetarian or eat only organic food. They are the biggest hypocrites around. I know someone who says they are vegetarian, yet every recycling day, their bin is full of pizza boxes, and I doubt it's a veggie pizza, and on numerous occasions I see McDonald's bags with lunch or dinner being carried into the house. That means I can say I am vegetarian because I eat meat, and most animals eat grass, plants.

Visits (Post-COVID)

It really did not sink in until COVID forced almost everyone to stay inside and be unable to do much of anything. There was no shopping at the malls, no eating out at local establishments, no trips to any family functions, no travelling anywhere, no participating in any activities, no visiting elders, no travelling to work. If you were lucky enough to work, chances were that you had to work from home at least part of the time. I cannot speak for everyone, but I really missed the interactions with other human beings. My dog Chelsea is great company, but it's not the same. Even before COVID, I went old school by going to a store to talk to someone, whereas most people would rather shop online and have something delivered to them. The same applies to a food store. People would rather go to self-checkout because it is a little faster. Sorry, but I prefer to say hello to a live person and share a few words during the transaction. If there is a smile during the transaction, even better.

It has been a long, long time that we have been unable to do the things we enjoy most, and that is enjoying life with family, friends, neighbours, and co-workers. I will say that I have never taken life for granted. It's a privilege to enjoy my short time on Earth because life can and has been taken away from people in a moment's notice. Maybe COVID can be a wake-up call to stop taking what we have assumed as an automatic way of life. Stop and appreciate what life allows us to have enjoy each and every day.

To some people (morons), it should be a kick in the ass because they have not done anything different during COVID, and they do nothing but bitch and complain about vaccines, masks, and social distancing. All I will say is, "Ignorance is bliss."

Once COVID restrictions are a thing of the past, I plan to start visiting family and friends on a regular basis because you never know what tomorrow will bring, and by then it could be too late.

Just a thought.

Why Mars (or, ET, Phone Home)

Are we really that infatuated with life on other planets that we forget what is happening right here on Earth? It puzzles me a little but irks me a lot.

Don't get me wrong, because I am all for advancement in technology, such as the electric car and solar panels, which help the environment. There is a curiosity about space exploration and extraterrestrial beings. But to me, what is being ignored or forgotten about is planet Earth, and right now it is something to seriously think about. There is so much money and other resources being spent on space, from all of the numerous experiments and expeditions to space stations to having a camera on Mars. The list goes on. My concern is the lack of funds, compassion, and caring to what is being left behind.

Look at the world today. There is so much famine, so much unnecessary death around the world, so much political unrest, so much fighting, so much racial injustice, and so much hate. But to me, equally important is looking at what we are doing to our planet. Numerous wildfires, earthquakes, tsunamis, volcano eruptions, tornadoes, hurricanes—you name it, and we have had it. Speaking of had it, that is what Mother Nature is telling us: she has had it with us and is giving us these challenges, which we are failing. These events are getting to be uncontrollable, and they seem to be getting closer in situations and more devastating to our world.

Climate change is affecting more than we think we know. Look at how wildlife is being affected. Look at the coral reefs, or lack thereof. We need these reefs to survive. Life is so dependent on the survival of these reefs.

Look at the rainforests, or lack of them. Wildfires and deforestation are reducing the oxygen in our atmosphere, which is so vital. Yeah, it's the same oxygen we breathe and that allows us to live. You should have figured it out by now, but the Earth is warming up more every year, and all of the good things in life we enjoy will start disappearing one by one, to the point of extinction. That also includes us.

In summary, why don't we concentrate on fixing this planet while we still can, before we colonize another planet that we can destroy as well?

Wood Puzzles (3D, That Is)

A while back, I was looking for something different to do with my downtime as a hobby. I was looking on the web one evening and came across this model that I did not know existed. I grew up building plastic models of cars and trucks that were put together with glue and then painted.

While I lived in Scarborough during the mid1960s, doing models and watching cartoons with my nephew Gerry on Saturday morning was a ritual. Then after I was separated in the late 1990s, in my condo with my three boys, Jason, Nicholas, and Andrew, Friday nights were model times again. A lot of talk and a lot of laughs were had by all.

Now, in my late sixties, I once again am doing models in my spare time. The difference is this time the models are made out of engineered, laser-cut wood, without glue—you just snap them together. Some have as many as six hundred pieces and can be complex. Even with the instructions that come with these models, they can be challenging. They can take as little as a day or several days, especially the large ones or when frustration sets in. I will quit for a while and come back later. One model had me so frustrated that a car engine went flying across my living room. Emphasis on the word *car* because if it was a plane engine, it might have been a method of trying it out. But no, I lost my patience and threw it across the room. I know it is an unacceptable act, but I honestly have learned patience.

Doing models teaches or improve the following:

1) Hand-eye coordination
2) Patience
3) Keeping the mind focused and the brain cells working
4) Motor skills
5) Problem-solving
6) Learning how to follow instructions
7) Self-esteem when the model is finished and works (some models have music boxes, clocks, lights, and more)

They should be used for therapy, for depression, for long days, and for anger management. I know they help me when I have a long day, a sad thought, or an isolated feeling when no one is around, and lately there have been more than I would like to name. But one bonus is that they make great gifts for grandchildren—you know, one-of-a-kind gifts just for them, from their grandfather.

I love originality, and these models sure are original. The variety is seemingly endless.

Writing a Song

A few years back, I thought it would be a unique idea to at least make an attempt at putting together some words, along with some notes. Then I would try to find someone with a little knowledge of recording, go out, and try to record a personal, one-of-a-kind song. A little help from friends (hint-hint, wink-wink) to make up a groupthink project would be helpful and fun.

Imagine people with diverse knowledge but with little or no musical ability, whether it be through singing or playing an instrument, trying to create a piece of art. It sure would be a challenge, but one worth trying to conquer. I am up for the challenge. If nothing else, the laughter would sure to dominate during the attempt. It could be a fun song, like the songs "Weird Al" Yankovic puts together. Change a few words around, and you have a completely new and different version, but now you can call it your own.

Singing or instrumental talent is not even in my vocabulary. Even when a small harmonica that I picked up from a well-known bookstore was put to my mouth, it sounded like nails on a chalkboard. Even my dog, who normally likes to be near me when I am the only one home, decided right away that she was out of here. Chelsea not only left the room I was in but went to the bedroom farthest away and disappeared under the bed, hiding under her blanket. When I went to look for her, she refused to come out. Needless to say, the harmonica is back in the original box and back on a shelf, collecting dust. There is a keyboard in the room I call my man room, but even that is collecting dust.

Back to my idea. If anyone out there would be willing to give me advice or volunteer to be part of this adventure, I am open to working with you. When I mentioned it to a couple of co-workers a while back, there was a hint of interest, so maybe I should put a little effort into seeking out local help first. And speaking of firsts, maybe I should first start trying to put down some words on paper to get started—kick myself in the ass to get motivated. You would be surprised at what you can accomplish when you put your mind to it. *Never* is a word that does not exist in my dictionary. Neither does the word *impossible*, but I will probably add that word once the mission is attempted. But then again, you never know what you can do once your mind is made up. I also love to be challenged.

Besides, as I am doing my own eulogy, it would be only fitting that I add the music to it as well. Another light bulb was just turned on. Now it is time to get started on this journey.

XO and XOXO

XO and XOXO are used at the end of a letter, a text, or an email. They are terms of endearment or a way of expressing affection towards others.

I think we all know what XO and XOXO mean, but I did not know how it was developed and when. Well, let me tell you that after a little research, I came up with the following.

Apparently, there is no clear-cut answer, but it is believed that the *X* comes from back in the Middle Ages, when people used to sign letters that way. *X* was used in place of a signature because many people could not read or write. It was also a Christian symbol meant to represent the cross, and it was used as a substitute for the word *Christ* by the way of the Greek Chi, which looks like an *X*. The theory is that because there is a long history of Christians kissing statues of Christ or the Bible, the *X* may have originally meant "seal it with a kiss." Another theory is that the *X* looks like two people kissing, and that's how it began to mean "kiss." Either way, by the mid-1800s, the meaning of *X* was solidified as "kiss."

Now for the *O*. It is believed to have come from Jewish immigrants who, also unable to read or write, arrived in North America and refused to sign documents with the Christian-associated *X*. Instead, they signed with an *O*. The *O* then made the jump to meaning "hug" simply as an opposite of *X*, which had already come to mean "kiss." The *O* also looks like two people hugging from above, so if we are going on the theory of appearances, that works just fine.

Regardless of the history of what XOXO really means, we are all familiar with the colloquial meaning now. That will wrap up my history lesson for the day. I will now go out and try to find someone who is also looking for XOXOs.

FYI, do not end any letter with XOX. That is a whole new meaning, and I am not even going to mention what it means. You can do your own research on that, but a word of advice: keep young children away if you do look up the meaning. I had no idea.

XPlane (Seriously)

The title is meant to be misspelled. The English language is so complex. Everyone talks about learning another language other than English. It can be extremely difficult, especially as we get older. Can you imagine trying to learn English?

I will give credit where credit is due. If I came from another country where English was not my first language, I would be so intimidated to have to learn the language, knowing how it is made up. Millions have done it, and a good majority speak the language and know the language better than those whose primary language is English. A great example would be former president (and yes, he is the former president) Donald Trump. Just look at how he spells words in his tweets. I know he is not the sharpest tool in the shed, but when he misspells words, everyone knows. That can be said about a lot of us, including me. How many times have you looked to the dictionary for help with the spelling of a word? Oh, sorry—a physical dictionary is antique today, because our computers tell us when we have misspelled a word, or wrongly use a word or phrase. It would be so much easier if we spelled words the way they sounded—you know, the phonetic way. Plus, why do certain words have different meanings? That adds to the confusion of the English language.

The following are two examples of what I mean about the craziness of English. There are thousands of others, but you get the picture. First is the spelling of words and simplified phonetic system used.

1. Telephone   Telafon
2. Elephant   Lefant

3.	Clean	Klen
4.	Heart	Hart
5.	Hockey	Hake
6.	Quick	Kwik
7.	Commercial	Cumrshl

Second is a list of words with different spellings or meaning.

V	Plane	Airborne object moving with wings
Adj.	Plane	Completely level or flat
N.	Plain	A large area of flat land with a few trees
N.	Plane	Tool with a projecting steel blade
N.	Plane	Tall, spreading tree of the northern hemisphere
Adj.	Plain	Not decorated or elaborate; simple in character
Adj.	Plain	Crystal clear
Adj.	Plain	Clearly, unequivocally (used for emphasis)
V	Ring	Make a clear, resonant, or vibrating sound
N	Ring	Act of causing a bell to sound
N	Ring	Call for service or attention
N	Ring	Enclosed space
V	Ring	Surround for protection or containment
N	Ring	A small, circular band of precious metal worn on a finger as an adornment or a token of marriage, engagement, or authority
V	Wring	Squeeze or twist
N	Wring	Act of squeezing or twisting
N	Ringer	A person or thing that looks exactly like another
N	Ringer	Professional playing an amateur sport
N	Ringer	Game of marbles
N	Ringer	A ring or similar object that is tossed to encircle a target (i.e., horseshoes)
N	Wringer	A device for wringing water from wet clothes
Adj.	Ringing	Emitting a clear, resonant sound
Adj.	Ringing	Forceful and unequivocal
Adj.	Wringing	Wrench or twist forcibly or painfully

These are just a couple of words that I thought of while writing this, and with a little help from my dictionary, I discovered the numerous meanings that these words have and the variance in spelling, although they are pronounced the same way.

I could write a book regarding the silliness of the English language, but life is too short to spend it making fun of the only language I understand. God bless those who have to learn to speak and understand the English language, because I don't think I could learn a new language. I still have trouble with English.

As an added note, it is also funny how when the same words are reversed in the same sentence, and the meaning can be totally different. The one example that comes to mind is taken from my favourite comedian, George Carlin. The infamous statement goes as follows: "You can prick your finger—just don't finger your prick." Only George could think of that. Genius.

Yearly Review

The concept of yearly review came to me about six years ago when, once again, I had nothing to do. I thought of this instead of going into a temporary hibernation mode, which means sitting in a recliner, lifting my feet, closing my eyes, and having a nap. Doing that is bad for two reasons. One is that it is a waste of time, having a snooze when life seems to fly by. But more importantly is the fact that I apparently snore, so I don't want to disturb anyone else in the house. I don't think that I snore, because I have never heard it. But back to my conceptual thinking at the time.

There was so much to do and so much to see, and the travel bug started to get to me. As I pondered where I wanted to go, I started thinking about what has been done in the past year so I could start a plan to make something happen not only for a trip but also for other things on my list. It's commonly known as the bucket list, but this one is a little smaller.

With proper planning, you can achieve anything you want, from a family reunion to a fundraising event, to a golf tournament, to a weekend getaway, to a family trip, to a trip to see family, to a sporting event, to (in my case) another safari.

Whatever you like to do takes effort, time, and patience. That's why I visit paperwork from the last year regarding travel to see how the trip went, so I can start planning the next adventure. No stone is left unturned, from where to go and why, to travel companies to work with, cost of the trip, cost of getting there, insurance, routes to get there, duration of stay, money to bring for my stay, vaccinations (if required), clothes, cameras, suitcases, lawn maintenance, security of home, and let's not forget work obligations and those who have to be asked to take us to and pick us up at the airport. Oh, and I am sorry, but in my case, I must not forget that I have to find someone to take care of my four-legged furry friend, Chelsea. So, as you can see, it takes a lot of planning, and that is why a paper trail may be necessary to alleviate some headaches and potential mistakes that could spoil the trip a little. Keeping records of whatever you have done of significant importance for future reference is important, no matter what it is. As I will vouch, it has helped me on numerous occasions. In the end, if you do not like the papers, purchase a shredder and have some fun. I then request that you find someone with a hamster or guinea pig to brighten up their home. As the saying goes, "Waste not, want not."

Yesterday

Yesterday is history,
Today is victory
Improve the present because tomorrow is still a mystery
—Adwika Vishal Jaiswal

No truer words have been said, but I would like to add a question: "Where in the hell did the time go?" Please excuse the explicit word, but time is going by at such an alarming rate. I am having trouble trying to catch my breath and keep up. It's like warp speed. I can still remember Sunday dinners with my parents while attending school, working to support myself, and playing hockey. After that, I remember getting married, buying my first house, being blessed with my first child (there would be four before all was said and done), and raising them, and watching them grow to the point where all four are now enjoying their next chapter with their own families. I am sitting here contemplating my next chapter, which means the word *retirement* has crossed my mind from time to time. That's it in a nutshell.

As a child, time goes by so slowly, but as that child grows, he or she soon realizes that time starts to pick up momentum to the point that by the time he or she has matured and grown into an adult, time is now in the express lane of the highway of life, and once there, it increases speed even more.

Although I cannot slow down the speed of life that I know that I am in the midst of, you can bet that I am going to also speed up what I have yet to see and do before I can no longer keep up with Father Time.

Periodically, I will reminisce and enjoy a recollection of many good times of the past, but at the same time, I think of what could have or should have done differently due to some unforced errors, as they say in tennis. But since that line of thinking cannot change the past, I will try to not only stay focussed on the good times of yesterday but also make improvements on today. On top of that, and more important, I work on enjoying the future by stopping putting plans aside until later, because those potential plans will also be part of yesterday quicker than you may think.

Yesterday is fun to go back to from time to time, but if you don't do some of your dreams now, there will be nothing to reminisce about later. My suggestion is to stop worrying about yesterday, plan today, and enjoy tomorrow. Because tomorrow never arrives, there is time to do a lot.

Zero Tolerance

I think of this from time to time on a lot of unrelated issues—from things that people do that are stupid or ignorant with respect to people's lives to acts of violence that change lives forever, to plain ignorance on a daily basis repeated over and over by the same person.

From the miniscule to the extreme, I have put my list of these acts (in no particular order), along with what I would consider a proper punishment. You may or may not agree, but hopefully it will open your eyes and your mind to these senseless acts, which are happening more and more every day. The first set are those that happen around the world seemingly on a daily basis lately. The second set are my personal pet peeves, and if I ever made it in politics at a local level, my first business would be to handle my (and probably others') issues with what I would call ignorance, stupidity, or both. Being elected to office is also on my bucket list.

Countrywide Issues

1. **Child molesters and sex offenders**
   Cut you-know-what off, and let them suffer while it heals on its own, if it heals at all. That way, they would have to think of what they did, like the victims do by suffering for a long time after with scars as a reminder.

2. **Drunk drivers**
   Put them on a race track and let a whole bunch of other drunk drivers' race, with the winner being the one who ends up hitting the convicted so as to reduce his charge.

3. Robbers

It's simple. If you steal anything, from a pencil to money or cars ...

- Minor offence: break the fingers on the hand that stole.
- Major offence: break both hands with no surgery to heal; as the adage goes, "An eye for an eye, a tooth for a tooth."
- If it is a car, the same applies to the foot.

4. Physical assault

Put the convicted into a ring with UFC fighters and let them fight their way out, one by one. It is not fair being outnumbered, plus the superior size, but maybe that should have been thought about before the assault.

5. Abused pets and wildlife killing

Again, it is simple: Put them in cages or tie them to a pole with a short chain. Leave them in the wide open and let them experience the extremes of weather where there is also no food and no water, and then walk away. They can be forgotten just like their animals. If they are killing for a sport, put the convicted in a wildlife environment with no weapons and walk away. Now, that would be a fair sport.

6. Abusive authorities

Put them in jail with not-so-nice convicts. You know—the ones who went against laws while on the outside. Now, let's see who has the authority in the cell, or while in the yard, or while eating in the dining area.

7. Murderers

Do unto me, and I shall do unto you, only I will do it so as not to hurt the others. The difference is the convicted will suffer to a slow death to think about what he or she has done and watch his or her family around in tears, just like the victim who has been killed.

8. Gun violence

There was talk that if convicted of possession of a firearm, it was an automatic ten-year sentence. I kind of like the concept of a ten-year sentence because although no one gets hurt, ten years is time to think about what possibly could happen. Whatever happened to the follow-up?

Or play a carnival game known as the *"Milk Bottle"* game where you put the bad guy on a shelf unable to move and then have someone shoot at him. Sometimes they miss, and sometimes they don't. I like that idea.

9. **Corporate leaders who abuse and lie**
   Take away all their assets and possessions and leave them with the clothes on their back. Throw them a used backpack or garbage bag and drop them off in a busy downtown core of hard-working people. No cell phone, no money, no credit cards, and no contact for assistance.

10. **Lying politicians**
    Put a dunce hat on their heads and force them to parade around publicly to show what they have done. Or even better, inject those politicians with Pinocchio serum. When they tell a lie, their nose grows longer with each lie.

On a Personal Note (Pet Peeves)

1. **Dog crapping on neighbour's lawn**
   Make the person do a walk around the community, and give him a scoop and a bag to pick up dog dodo for a few weeks. Make him wear a sandwich sign to show neighbours his bad habit. Or do what I did: put his dog's poop on his door step.

2. **Children making noise at all hours**
   Have parents volunteer in an overcrowded, understaffed day care, especially after doing a hard day of work. Or force them to supervise a children's party at McDonald's or Chuck E. Cheese.

3. **Homeowners with backyard parties past midnight**

   Have neighbours collectively have their lawnmowers going up and down the fence of the noisemaker's house, and follow up with a whipper snipper along with loud music to enjoy while doing yard duties. The earlier in the day, the better.

4. **Cars with noisy mufflers driving up and down residential streets**

   Let them drive on residential streets, and have those spike strips unexpectedly appear. Or maybe use duct tape or gorilla glue on the muffler and force the noise inside the car with the windows up.

5. **People parking in the handicap spot**

   Make the convicted park at the farthest point of entry, tie their hands and legs together, and then let them attempt to go in to buy something. Watch them try to carry it back to their car. Put it on video and show it on YouTube.

6. **Not following protocol during the COVID crisis**

   Force these ignorant people to volunteer in the ICU or other wards of a hospital, where there is potential for germs spreading, while they wear only underwear and a T-shirt.

7. **Drivers with no respect for laws**

   Put these drivers in a car with a maximum speed of twenty kilometres per hour and put them in rush-hour traffic. Or put them in the same car in a demolition derby and see if they can escape unharmed.

8. **People who throw their cigarette butts on the sidewalk or private property**

   Make them walk in a busy downtown core with a pooper scooper to clean up all the butts. Or have some people in his neighbourhood come by the smoker's house and put their butts in his car. Let him get rid of the stench of the butts.

9. **People who advertise business on community mailboxes**

   Put larger signs and notices on the advertiser's house to show them how tacky and cheap it is, not to mention what an eyesore it is. Let's also use duct tape to hold the signs, and when taking them down, let the paint peel off to show the aftermath and destruction of private property

10. **People who talk on their phone at the same time they are ordering fast food**

    Force the person to go on the other side of the counter and try to take the order from similar people who are ignorant of the hard-working people who serve us. Maybe at a place right next to a high school. That will show them what they have to put up with.

Zip-a-Dee-Doo-Dah

This is a fun little song that I have sung from time to time. Whether in a good mood or not in a good mood, to me, it's a pick-me-up that puts me in a better mood, no matter what I am feeling or the situation I am in.

The song was composed by Allie Wrubel, with lyrics provided by Ray Gilbert, and it was sung by James Baskett in the 1946 Disney movie *Song of the South*.

Unfortunately, it's been called a little racist by some who feel slavery was exposed during the movie, and Disney has pulled the movie from view and locked it away so it cannot be seen.

I sing it with no ill intent, just to feel a little better. Maybe you should try it. But be careful, because it can be addictive. Just like the chip commercial— you know the one: "Bet you can't eat just one."

I have included a few lines from the lyrics for your viewing pleasure.

> Zip-a-dee-do-dah, zip-a-dee-ay
> My, oh my, what a wonderful day
> Plenty of sunshine headin' my way
> Zip-a-dee-do-dah, zip-a-dee-ay
>
> Mister Bluebird's on my shoulder
> It's the truth, it's actual
> Everything is satisfactual

Final Thoughts

My simple yet honest writings are all based on observations by keeping my eyes open, my ears open, and my mouth shut. Life is a long journey of learning. It took me a long time to learn that, but when I did, life started to become more meaningful, more fulfilling, and more worthwhile. Heck, even laughter became easier. Every day I learn something new, regardless of how miniscule it may be. It could be beneficial, inspirational, or simply put a smile on my face.

I hope that I have come across that way with these short stories for your interest, along with a sense of humour. I enjoy putting a smile on the faces of people close to me. It makes my day a lot better.

To my family, friends, and co-workers, I would like to thank you for your support, patience, and understanding during the good times and some not-so-good times. I have been blessed to be around some of the hardest working, family oriented, humorous people who have made my life a rewarding one, and I look forward to seeing you and sharing stories or a few laughs on a daily basis or whenever time permits.

In closing, life is what you make of it. Be your own person and do the things that make you happy. You would be surprised how people will respond. I encourage you to not only live your dream but also help or influence others to do something for themselves. And that's what life is all about, isn't it? By giving, you receive. That is a great way to be happy.

Now that I have completed the task of writing short topics of how to enjoy every day with the letters *A* to *Z*, I will now officially put down my pen, enjoy my favourite snack, and drink before I retire for the night—and that drink is a large glass of milk along with a few cookies. That's been a staple with me since I was a child, and I still enjoy it today. Nothing beats it. I hope that my children can learn to enjoy every day because life is so short. And who wants to be miserable, anyway?

As I leave my room to scamper downstairs and prepare my snack, I wish everyone a saying that I remember from a television show when I was young, *The Red Skelton Show*. The last line at the end of his show was, "Good night, and may God bless." It simply means an expression of gratitude, love, and laughter. It is short in words but long in meaning.

Printed in the United States
by Baker & Taylor Publisher Services